Running

Slim and Fit with The Right Exercise Programme

CONTENTS

Slim and Fit with the Right Exercise Programme

Disclaimer

All possible care has been taken by the author in compiling the information contained in this book and by the publisher in checking its accuracy. Nonetheless, no liability can be assumed for possible errors contained in the book. Neither the author nor the publisher can be held responsible for the accuracy of the information in this book or for possible damages resulting from such information.

Picture credits: J. Bodemer p. 57; CMA p. 42, 44f, 46; J. Enneper p. 23, 77, 78, 81, 82 (2), 83, 84, 86; Falke p. 36; Currex/B. Gustafsson p. 29, 32 (2); FIT for LIFE p. 92; Fotolris p. 55; Ryffel-Running p. 8, 89; Spomedis p. 10, 22/23 (2), 49; W. Stinn p. 6, 20/21 (2), 22

The illustrations and descriptions of the exercises as well as portions of the text on pages 66–69 and 72–76 are from the pamphlet *Marathon leicht gemacht* ("Marathons Made Easy"), released by the Swiss magazine for endurance sports *FIT for LIFE*, in co-operation with Ryffel-Running. The exercises with an elastic band on pages 70f stem from Ludwig Artzt GmbH, Agents of Medical Technology, Hadamar, Germany.

The publisher would also like to thank the firms Asics, CamelBak, Currex, Falke, Gore, Nike, Odlo, Polar Electro, Reebok, Sugoi, Tao, and the CMA as well as TUI AG (p. 47, 23) for friendly permission to reproduce numerous photographs and access to informational materials.

© Naumann & Göbel Verlagsgesellschaft mbH, a subsidiary of VEMAG Verlags- und Medien Aktiengesellschaft, Cologne

Author: Jens Bodemer
Translation from German to English: Markus Flatscher
Complete production: Naumann & Göbel Verlagsgesellschaft mbH, Cologne
Printed in China

ISBN 3-625-10364-8

CONTENTS

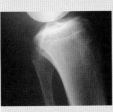

RUNNING – A WONDERFUL CHALLENGE ...

*H*ave you ever wondered at how many people nowadays manage to run a marathon? All over the world, weekend after weekend, an ever-increasing number of people take on this challenge, even though it is not entirely without risk. Why is this? Among citizens of the Western hemisphere, the marathon has become an adventure that ranks among the top things people would like to experience at least once in their lifetimes.

The Emil Zatopek Memorial is located in the Park of the International Olympic Committee (IOC) in Lausanne.

"If you want to run, run a mile. But if you want to experience an entirely new life, run a marathon!"
This concise description of the marathon experience stems from none other than Emil Zatopek, also known as the "Czech locomotive", the incredible runner and multiple Olympic champion, and he really couldn't have described it any better.

The historical origins of the marathon are shrouded in legend. The story begins with the death of an ancient athlete who died as a result of running from Marathon to Athens in order

to deliver the message of a Greek victory over the Persians. And yet that original distance was not even as long as today's 26 miles and 385 yards. During the 1908 Olympic games in London, the British Queen ordered the distance extended by 385 yards, so that the runners would have to pass by the Royal Box. This led to the modern distance, which is still valid to this day.

Today, the mythical marathon has turned into a symbol for the modern, prosperous citizen, who takes the ancient challenge in order to connect with the heroic. Indeed, a marathon requires all the qualities that count in today's achievement-oriented society: persistence, strength, stamina, motivation, patience, good self-assessment and, last but not least, the ability to endure something painful in order to come out stronger than before. And just as in other aspects of life, the marathon's special appeal lies in the fact that you never know for sure in advance: the surprise effect can be intense, since your performance partly depends on luck and the shape you are in on a given day. This adds further to the fascination of an actually quite predictable challenge.

10 Million Joggers in the UK

*R*unning 26.2 miles (42.195 km) on asphalt may not be a particularly healthy thing to do, but training for a marathon certainly is. In the UK alone, there are almost 10 million joggers. This doesn't mean that all of them are running marathons – why should they? Running three to seven miles three times a week is better for your health. However, once you have made a habit of running regularly, you may find that you want more. If that happens, you'll know that you're among the growing number of people who have been bitten by the exercise bug.

Marathon as a party: city runs have been reporting two-digit growth rates for years – a steady trend with no end in sight. Even so, marathon runners are only the tip of the iceberg when it comes to running aficionados.

Have you ever asked yourself how long it is going to be until you, too, complete a marathon? It doesn't matter how much you currently weigh, what you look like, how old you are, or even if you have never seriously exercised in your entire life thus far. Everyone can do it! You, too, are capable of running a marathon.

Does that sound like a dream? It could be more than that in less than a year's time. In any case, such an undertaking is a great challenge.

Using sample exercises, this book will show you what an individual training program, tailored to your particular situation and to your personal constitution, might look like. You're going to receive a lot of tips on what to look out for on your way to a more healthy life by practicing the most natural of all sports. If you already are an amateur runner, you will find lots of new information on how to devise a systematic and effective exercise program, especially if you want to add a purpose and a goal to your hobby. Bungee jumping was yesterday. The kick you get out of a marathon lasts much longer – indeed, for most finishers, it lasts for a lifetime.

Starting your day earlier than others with a sunrise run will make you radiate with self-confidence the whole day long. A new, uplifting lifestyle!

… AND THE BEST MEDICINE

Overweight people participate in ultra-runs, such as the one in Iceland shown above. Running is the proper sport for everyone willing to do something for their bodies and sense of well-being.

The typical distribution of diseases overweight people suffer from:

People eat too much sugar, too much fat, and generally too much of everything. They do not exercise enough and drink too much alcohol." This is the scathing upshot of a European government's nutrition report in 2004. This general trend began in the 1960s, with the great improvement in our standard of living. It would seem that we haven't learned much in the ensuing four decades; we still suffer from too much affluence, in spite of a slackening economy. The fact is that, given the less abundant food supply in earlier generations, there were considerably less cardio-vascular and civilisation diseases such as type 2 diabetes, sometimes referred to as "lifestyle diabetes", which can be triggered by the kind of lifestyle sketched in the quotation above.

The fact that more than 50 % of all Western adults are over-weight is not the only thing that's alarming – this trend applies to children, too. Amongst children aged 6 to 18, obesity has doubled in the past 20 years. We all know the reasons: too much candy, and joysticks and computer games instead of outdoor play. Early in their lives, kids are already geared toward become couch potatoes. Like the average day for most adults, our children's days are defined by a "seat cycle": breakfast table, car or bus, desk chair, lunch table, desk chair, car seat, TV, bed. The cycle repeats day after day, week after week, month after month, year after year. This is in direct contrast to our physical needs, since the human body has been programmed to be in motion to forage for thousands of years. Just like our ancestors', our bodies store fat. Today, however, they are no longer used up, since periods of hunger and the necessity to hunt for food no longer exist. How often do

Most frequent diseases found in overweight people

85 %	diabetes	53 %	degenerative diseases of joints and skeleton
80 %	hyperlipemia		
70 %	gout		
60 %	heart insufficiency	50 %	hypertonia

we even have to walk a distance worth mentioning and really use our muscle power anymore? Not too often, right? Maybe on holiday – but even then, we often take it easy. After all, the more we refrain from exercises, the more effort it requires to get up and going again! The same applies to life itself. In the past, man was a running hunter. Today, in order to preserve our health, we have to simulate the hunt for food. And we are infinitely better off than our ancestors: we are free to choose when and how far we want to run. We can run without the pressure our ancestors experienced; we can run for relaxation, to let go of our everyday worries. Even so, more often than not, we just don't do it. Instead we reward ourselves for a long day at work by sitting down and having an opulent meal, eating more than our sense of hunger is telling us to, out of mere appetite and hedonism. After all, we deserve it – or so we think, even though what our body actually deserves is some exercise.

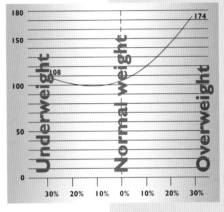

Mortality rate (chart shows values in percentage), clearly illustrating lower mortality for slightly underweight persons and a rapid increase proportional to weight.

Losing Weight Becomes Easy

What would you say if we told you that losing weight is actually easy? That you'll be able to eat whatever you want, as much you want, as soon as you have made a commitment to your personal roadmap to health by relying on the most natural of all patterns of movement: running? Your appetite will change automatically. If you are running to the point where you experience an oxygen rush, your body will release cholecysto-kinin, an enzyme that signals "I am full". Running will become part of your daily routine, just like personal hygiene, because it will make you feel better. Say goodbye to feeling lazy and listless. Running doubles your oxygen supply, giving you more energy and more joy. Running is living.

Sharpen Your Senses

Harmonise yourself with nature: enjoy running through autumn foliage and experience the beautiful colours.

As you become fitter you will rediscover your senses; even your sense of taste will improve. You'll experience the four seasons more distinctly: think of the cool and warm spots in a forest in springtime, some still covered with rotting foliage, while grass sprouts elsewhere. Think of the warmth on your skin after the

initial chill after a swim in summer, or the cooling effect of sweat in the glistening sun. Think of trees shimmering red in the autumn sun, and the swishing noise when you jog on the first fallen leaves. Or think of short winter days when you take a brisk walk in the crystal-clear, crisp winter air and snow crunches beneath your feet. As a runner, you experience these things much more frequently than others who don't exercise regularly out of doors.

Running – The Simplest of All Sports

If you feel that running is too much of a strain, simply start walking. You will soon experience a desire to run.

Trend sports are great – especially for the sports industry. Your new golf equipment might not contribute much to your health, but to your soul, instead. You are proud of being part of the golfing set. However, there is an easier way: leave behind the trodden paths of technological mobility and make a commitment to greater fitness, health, and a higher quality of life. Leave your car if the distance is short. Take a step, take a walk. It is never too late – not even if you had to wait for retirement to find time to do yourself some good. You are worth it! Just start walking, and soon you will experience a desire to run. If you start out slowly and don't rush things, your body will soon thank you for it. However, you will need to have a little patience. The initial outings will take some effort. This is the very reason why half of all beginners quit again, true to the biblical saying: the spirit is willing, but the flesh is weak. Stick it out and keep trying.

You will see: it is worth the effort. Soon you will be addicted – in the most positive sense of the word – to your daily bit of freedom. Just start running and enjoy the break.

Sticking with It While Keeping It Fun

- Set realistic targets for yourself (read more about this on page 50).
- Take care not to overstrain yourself, and don't be too hard on yourself – after all, this is about improving your health, not setting records.
- Plan your training schedule according to your own goals, not according to others. Keep in mind work and time issues.
- Still, exercise regularly and keep your exercise varied (try other sports, too). Make sure to allow for necessary rest periods.
- Even if you do not have time to exercise frequently, make sure not to train too hard in one session.
- Allow for variation by adapting to the given situation: exercise at different hours of the day, for example, or try different endurance sports according to the season, such as swimming in summer or cross-country skiing in winter. When you don't feel like running, try Nordic Walking for a change.

Fight weariness and a lack of motivation with variation: Nordic Walking also exercises your arm muscles.

If you keep these few pieces of advice in mind, you will get through the occasional spell of low motivation, and running will become fun – and stay fun. Keep in mind, as a beginner, it will only take a committment of half a year in order to completely change your life. Wouldn't you say that this is a great incentive and makes it worth sticking it out? As soon as you understand what's going to happen to your body, you won't want to waste another day before beginning your individual training program.

What Will Happen to Your Body

*F*rom the very beginning of your new activity level, you will activate your vegetative nervous system, establishing a balance between exercise and active relaxation. Your body will take the break it needs in order to reorganise your metabolism. You will notice that your sleep becomes deeper.

Next, your blood will respond: "good" and "bad" cholesterol (HDL and LDL values, respectively) will be more balanced. Next up is the cardiovascular system: high blood pressure is lowered after only a couple of weeks of regular running, because the fluidity of your blood is improved. This also decreases the risk of strokes and heart attacks, since their major cause is agglutination (thrombus formation and the narrowing of blood vessels by plaque deposits).

A firm body is just the outwardly visible consequence of organs made healthy through running.

And without even noticing, you may have already lost a couple of pounds. You can take pride in this success. After many years of ongoing endurance training, your skin will become thinner and feel softer as the fat content of the subcutis layer melts away, and in some places, muscles and sinews will become distinctly visible on your arms and legs – a great feeling. Your kinaesthetic sense will also im-

prove. Your sense of movement, coordination and posture in everyday life will be enhanced, as well. What is more, you will soon begin to feel things that are not immediately obvious on the outside: your immune system will be stronger. Exercising temporarily creates tissue stress, which results in a reaction of the immune system. As a by-product of endurance training, highly competent immune cells (the natural killer cells) activate repair mechanisms which also fend off viruses and germs. Cancer cells are also among the structures these cells recognise as extraneous. In this respect, moderate endurance training (40–45 minutes, about four times a week) also provides natural protection against certain kinds of cancer. On average, your immune system's performance will be increased by 50 per cent.

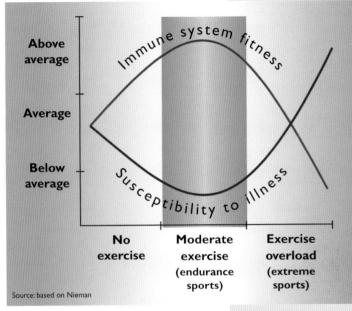

Source: based on Nieman

This "fish curve" illustrates the dynamics of susceptibility to infections as correlated with exercise: while moderate exercise strengthens our immune system, susceptibility to infections is increased when we exercise too little or even too much.

As soon as you have established your own personal training rhythm and a suitable balance of training and relaxation, your body will begin to release endorphins, chemicals which will increase your motivation and ability to function under pressure in other areas of life, too. You will literally run off your everyday stress. Moreover, the right dose of exercise will make your sex hormones dance: moderate exercise boosts sexual pleasure, while too much or too little exercise tends to reduce libido (read more on page 50).

Weight training boosts testosterone levels – great not only for the libido, but for your bones, as well.

Here again, in order to establish the most effective rhythm and balance, it's important that you make variety a key element of your training. Especially in weight training, short and intense exercise sessions alternating with long pauses will cause your body to release the highest levels of testosterone, the male sex hormone. However, one-sided training of this kind has its limitations, as the necessary level of blood circulation is not maintained over time. Achieving and maintaining that level requires regular endurance training.

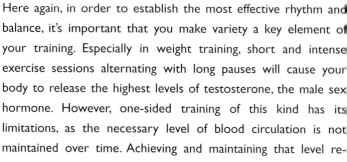

Obviously, all these positive benefits will only come about if you exercise in the appropriate way. This book is going to show you how to do this. It will enable you to take the first steps on your own. Alternatively, you may wish to join a group. Also, it may help to have a personal coach. You'll quickly find out if the chemistry between you is right, and with the knowledge presented in the remainder of this book, you'll be able to assess their competence and experience.

Before You Start Running

Before you begin training, you should definitely get a medical check-up, especially a cardiovascular check.

This check-up should include:
- Routine blood tests (laboratory report)
- Both rest and stress ECGs
- Blood pressure controls (resting and during exercise)

The check-up may also include an orthopaedic examination, especially if there are any known defects in your musculo-skeletal system.

An initial check-up is particularly important for those who belong to certain risk groups:

- Smokers
- People aged 36+
- Sports beginners or anyone resuming exercise after 2–3 years of abstinence from athletic activities
- Those with a history of defects in their spines or joints
- People with high blood pressure, diabetes or who are overweight

During an acute illness (even one as simple as a common cold), and especially when you have a fever, you must not run at all! Keep an eye on your resting heart rate as you recover, and resume running slowly and gradually.

Trail running is the perfect preparation for cross-country runs.

*D*on't start by trying to take your third step before the first one. Slowly accustom yourself to the fascination of running and marathons by enjoying some beautiful, easy runs first. It is a good thing to have a goal to look forward to, but keep that goal in the back of your mind at first. You still have a long way to go.

RUNNING AND MARATHONS

Enjoy these pictures as a source of motivation. Immerse yourself in the world of running. At first, the reward is in the journey. Your first marathon or half-marathon will happen soon enough. Let yourself be inspired by these scenic and mountain runs, city marathons and trails along the world's most beautiful coasts.

The Interlaken Jungfrau Marathon on the Kleine Scheidegg Mountain is considered one of the best organised mountain marathons. The ascent offers a view of the impressive Eiger North Face.

For a lot of amateur runners who don't want to conquer the cities, trail running is the new challenge of choice. With a water bottle and some snacks in their backpacks, it's almost like hiking. When choosing your backpack, make sure to get a model with an abdominal belt, so you can jog freely without the bag bouncing around.

Today there are a number of well organised cross-country and mountain runs that offer an opportunity to rise to the challenge of a trail run. The picture at the left was taken at the Matterhorn run.

The Großglockner mountain race course leads along glaciers, literally over rocks and boulders.

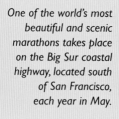

One of the world's most beautiful and scenic marathons takes place on the Big Sur coastal highway, located south of San Francisco, each year in May.

A run near the village of St. Wolfgang with Schafberg Mountain in the background.

Festive atmosphere at the starting line: from the very start, runners feel like winners.

A run on the beach, against the backdrop of the Golden Gate Bridge in the San Francisco Bay Area.

Barefoot on asphalt: impressions from the Cologne marathon recall the Carneval season.

The TUI Majorca Marathon is often more about sightseeing than about setting personal records. Many runners participate mainly to combine a run with a vacation on the beach.

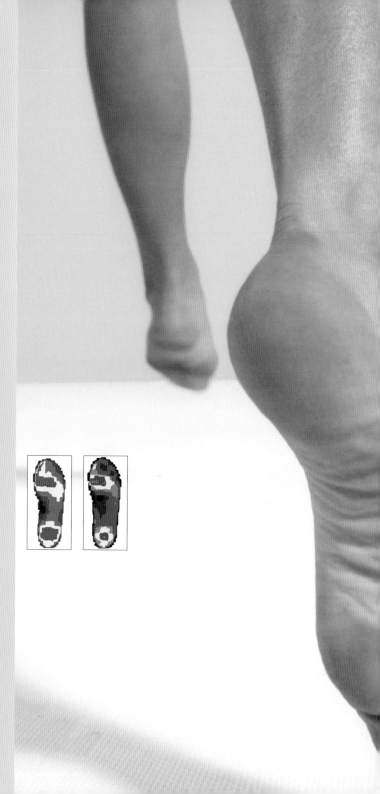

These infrared pressure profiles illustrates how pressure points are more evenly distributed when running barefoot (left image). Thick rubber soles may be very comfortable, but they do not accurately map the foot's natural shock absorbance system. Wearing shoes, the impact forces are more localised than when running barefoot

SIMPLY START RUNNING?

Basic Anatomy

*B*efore you start thinking about the right running shoe, you should have some general idea of the motion sequence that occurrs when your foot hits the ground. Generally speaking, your foot already is a shock absorber.

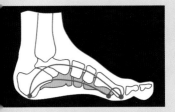 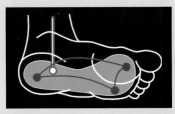

The anatomy of the foot is characterised by two longitudinal and one transverse arch. The calcaneus and the heads of the first and fifth metatarsals are exposed to the highest impact forces.

Your Foot is a Shock Absorber

This is especially true when the forefoot is used actively, because this is the only way to ensure that the calf muscle is able to perform its absorbing function in order to protect the knee joint from shocks. In the case of healthy foot biomechanics, the foot should roll inwards four to eight degrees – this is called pronation. This movement deflects the enormous impact forces over the entire sole of the foot, serving as a natural shock absorbance system for our feet. Moreover, this mechanism allows the foot to adapt to the terrain at hand and helps us maintain our balance.

Foot Types

*T*he human foot consists of 28 bones, 114 ligaments and 20 muscles. The bones are divided into tarsal bones, metatarsals and phalanges. Together, they construct a hollow space just above the ground, whose stability depends on the strength of the muscles and ligaments. The foot's longitudinal arch extends from the heel to the basal joint of the big toe, the ball of the foot.

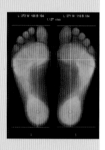

Normal foot: The image to the left shows a normally formed arch. The heel and forefoot are connected by a relatively broad surface functioning as the outward impact area. When running, the foot hits the ground on the outside and then rolls inward (natural pronation) in order to deflect the impact. Runners with a normal foot type do not need running shoes with strong motion controlling or stabilising supports.

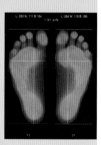

Flatfoot: This imprint shows a broader impact area. The arch is almost not present, or is not functional, because it is almost completely pressed to the ground. This may result from overweight or simply from one's anatomy. The sagging longitudinal arch causes the foot to roll inward, or over-pronate, and thus unable to absorb the shock properly. This is compensated for elsewhere, at the knee or hip, for instance, and results in motion compensation and potential overload – a typical indication for motion control shoes.

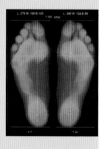

High arched foot: In the case of a high arched foot, the heel and the ball of the foot are connected only by a narrow area (as shown left). While this does not cause pronation problems, the foot itself does not have enough natural pronation to absorb shock. Shoes, therefore, must be softer and compensate for the lack of this natural function. A shoe with a stiff anti-pronation block on the inside would be the wrong choice in this case.

The Motion Sequence of Slow and Easy Jogging

Heel strike phase: Every time the foot strikes the ground as we walk or run, it has to handle a severe impact. The shock is deflected by the heel bone, generating a force three to five times the body's weight. The midsole and the absorbing elements in the heel of a shoe deflect and absorb the impact during strike phase, which reduces the stress placed on the foot and thereby extends the length of time we can run before tiring.

Roll-through phase: During this phase, the forces generated on impact are deflected from the heel to the balls of the smaller toes and, following pronation, come to rest mainly on the ball of the foot after pronation. At this point, the whole foot carries the body's weight.

Keeping your stride close to your centre of gravity or, in other words, making sure you don't take overly large steps, will significantly reduce the force of impact and braking.

Push-off phase: The body's weight is shifted from the forefoot to the balls of the toes, and on to the toes themselves, which spread apart in the process. During this phase, the forces increase to four to seven times the body's weight. By contraction of the calf muscle, the accessory and the toe flexors, the body is moved forward until the foot is lifted again for the next step. During this phase, the running shoe must optimally assist the foot's push-off motion. This is ensured by high flexibility and moderate absorbance support to

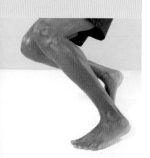

the forefoot. Moreover, natural pronation must not be constricted by overly strong support elements in the medial (inner metatarsus) and lateral (outward) regions.

Choosing the Right Shoe

*E*ven though some experts quite rightly advocate running barefoot as a means to strengthen the foot, at least for therapeutic reasons, for the vast majority of runners, their footgear remains the most important piece of equipment both for working out and for competition. After all, a wide variety of surfaces have to be dealt with, ranging from forest soil to open terrain to asphalt, and the various kinds of impact forces acting on the body have to be counteracted. However, the range of running shoes available is vast, and it can be difficult for lay-persons to choose the shoe type that's optimal for them. To help you make sense of the options, the following section gives an overview of the most important types of running shoes.

You may be able to exercise barefoot in your living room year round, but not in mud and ice. Adequate footwear is a must.

Basic Shoe Types

Shock absorbent: This type of shoe is designed to help absorb impact forces acting from below while maintaining the foot's natural flexibility during the roll-through.

Stabilising: In case of insufficiently stable ankle joints, your running shoes should feature stabilising elements in order to prevent extreme postures (e.g., over-pronation). Stabilising running shoes are recommended in particular for people who are overweight.

Motion Control: Runners whose foot motion patterns have to be stabilised because of biomechanical weaknesses use this type of shoe. Shoes like this have a stable base and contain visible elements that help control foot motion. It should be noted, however, that excessive control can be harmful, as it forces the natural sequence of motions into a particular pattern and may even aggravate individual weaknesses. For this reason, some manufacturers have discontinued making these models. In case of musculoskeletal anomalies, it is advisable to rely on individually customised orthopaedic inserts cast from plaster or foam, which are also available on prescription.

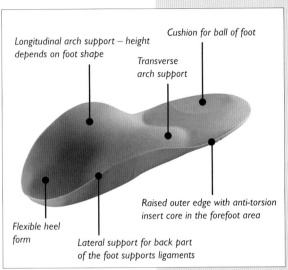

Longitudinal arch support – height depends on foot shape

Cushion for ball of foot

Transverse arch support

Raised outer edge with anti-torsion insert core in the forefoot area

Flexible heel form

Lateral support for back part of the foot supports ligaments

Elements of good sports inserts.

Lightweight Shoes: Particularly lightweight shoes are used for speed workouts and for competition. While they provide a high degree of flexibility, they do not provide strong shock absorbance or stabilization. This type of shoe is built with a strongly curved last. The curved shape counteracts pronation without providing any additional supporting function. This makes the shoe especially suitable for speedy, quick ground contact and for experienced, lightweight competitive runners. Casual runners carrying a few extra pounds are advised against buying this type of shoe – or at least, they should not set off on a street race of 6-plus miles, but instead let the body gradually grow accustomed to the feel of running with lightweight shoes.

All-round models: This type is a combination of the variations explained above. All-round shoes frequently have a simple structure and are lighter than stabilising shoes, which makes them an interesting alternative or second model. Every runner should own two pairs of shoes anyway: changing between them results in different distributions of impact and pressure points on the foot, giving them a chance to rest. An all-round model is also suitable for beginners.

One More Piece Of Advice:
Especially in 10K races, many runners use shoes that are much too hard, risking sore muscles even while running. Harder shoes do serve a purpose: while softer shoes tend to shut down the receptors in the joints, harder ones do not. However, the kinds of shoes competitive runners often request from shoe manufacturers are completely unsuitable for casual runners; after all, these professional running shoes are too lightweight and hardly provide any support. What is more, their shock absorbance level is too low for a casual runner's gait. Casual runners have longer periods of contact with the ground, resulting in greater weight on the foot, and therefore need better absorbance that helps to deflect impact forces and shocks that occur when the foot strikes asphalt. So, if you are a beginner, do not buy professional, competitive running shoes for your first race.

Movement Tendency Check

*N*ow that you as a potential customer are aware of the various functions of running shoes, and you're in a position to make an informed preselection, it is important to find out about your individual characteristics, e.g. with regard to your roll-through profile or any possible overweight. There are special shoes that aim to compensate for different types of abnormal

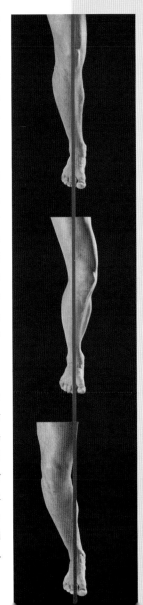

roll-through patterns, for straining forces on ligament structures and for defective positions of ankle joints. There is a simple test to determine your individual foot posture. Just stand on one leg while barefoot and bend your knee, and your knee will show your personal motion tendency:

Normal foot: The knee of a runner with an ideal, healthy foot position will be vertically aligned with the ball of the foot, but will tilt inward during over-pronation and outward during supination. This is the result of the runner trying to keep his or her balance by leveraging the knee to compensate for the inconvenient posture.

Over-pronation: When the foot tilts too far inward during roll-through (illustrated in the middle picture, showing a flatfoot) this is called over-pronation. Over-pronation results in a loss of natural lateral stability. The strong inward motion of the ankle joints is compensated for by the knee, frequently leading to damage of that joint over time. Therefore, runners with this common problem often have to wear a shoe with special stabilising elements in the interior area in order to minimise the foot's over-pronation.

Supination: Supination, or under-pronation, is when the foot rolls forward along the outside edge, thereby diminishing the natural shock absorbance of the longitudinal arch. This also leads to a loss of lateral stability and increases the risk of injuries caused by outward twists of the ankle. A supinator usually has a high arched foot, and the arch is inflexible, resulting in a reduced capacity of the foot to fulfil its natural shock-absorbing function. Therefore, this type of run-

31

 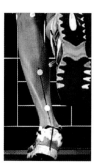

Barefoot supination (l) and pronation of a foot wearing a shoe that is too soft in the medial area.

ner needs a flexible, cushioned shoe with no medial post. For each type of runner, there are special shoes that counteract the motion pattern and compensate for less-than-ideal foot postures.

Determine Your Shoe Size

One factor not to be underestimated in choosing your running shoes is the proper shoe size:

During roll-through, you will quickly realise that your toes touch the tip of the toe box even though there seems to be plenty of room when you are standing. Shoes that seem to fit often are actually too tight and can lead to painful conditions of onychia and inflammations of the ball of the foot.

1. There should be a space the width of a thumb in between the tip of the shoe and your big toe.
2. When the foot is bent during push-off, the shoe is compressed, causing your toes to move forward quite a bit.
3. When the toes push off, the foot spreads to the side. If you choose shoes that are too tight, your toes will not have enough room during this phase, which can cause pain, areas of friction, blisters, and burning on the soles.

As a matter of principle, a running shoe should fit perfectly at the heel and in the medial area, forming a stable belt around the heel bone.

The Right Shoe Last Form

Shoes used for different purposes need different forms. You should therefore pay attention to the form of the lasts. Competitive running shoes, for instance, are strongly curved, allowing for a quick transition from the foot to the toes. Motion control shoes, on the other hand, have a straight last, giving the runner a larger surface area and higher stability.

Standard last: This last is for runners with normal feet who need a shoe that falls in the mid-spectrum in terms of both cushioning and stability. This shoe type's semi-curved last also makes it a good choice for neutral runners and slight over-pronators.

Straight last: A straight last provides the highest degree of control to runners who tend towards excessive over-pronation as a result of overly flat feet. This type of shoe's broad sole offers extra stability and control.

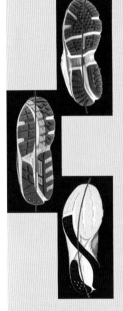

Curved last: This last provides very little stability, but it's highly flexible and encourages quick transitional movements throughout the phases of the running gait. A curved gives both joggers and ambitious runners a particularly dynamic roll-off.

A Special Tip for Women

Knock knees are common among women because women's femurs are connected to the pelvis at a higher point than men's. This leads to a greater frequency of over-pronation. In addition, women tend to have a smaller heel, and their metatarsals are usually higher and smaller than men's. Therefore, women's shoes have special lasts that are designed for women, and they are generally designed to fit smaller feet, thus combining stability with a better fit.

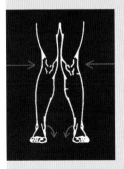

Clothes Make the Runner

Running in any weather – in clothing that's water-proof on the outside, yet breathable.

"There's no such thing as bad weather, there's only bad clothing," goes a popular saying. You may ask yourself what functions running fabric actually has to perform. The most important features of any running outfit are **weight, waterproofness, wind resistance and breathability**. No garment can meet all these criteria 100 per cent; what is most important is what type of runner you are and of course in what weather conditions you will be running. Choosing adequate, well-fitting clothes allows you to fully enjoy the running experience. Moreover, modern and functional clothes have a wide range of additional benefits: they're comfortable, robust, easy to clean, dry quickly, lightweight, soft, pleasant to wear next to the skin, and sometimes antibacterial and therefore odourless.

Wicking of Moisture: when we exert ourselves the body's temperature rises and glands in the skin produce sweat. Your good old cotton shirt can become drenched and stick to your skin, which is especially uncomfortable when it's chilly outside. Modern sportswear helps moisture evaporate more quickly. The fabrics themselves dry faster, making the person wearing them feel more comfortable. The energy that the body would otherwise use for thermo-regulation (i.e., for keeping its temperature at a constant level) is made available for the athletic effort and gain.

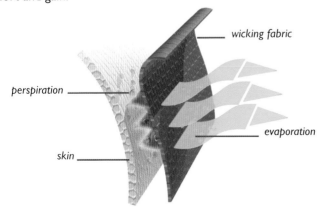

perspiration

wicking fabric

evaporation

skin

Modern fabrics ensure quick evaporation of sweat away from your body.

Comfort: Running clothes should offer optimal wearing comfort. Naturally, they have to allow for maximum freedom of movement, thus contributing to the athlete's ease in motion and comfort. Particularly soft and cosy fabrics not only feel nice, they also prevent rubbing and scouring of the clothes against the skin.

Smart Looks: There's more to clothes than mere functionality, and this applies to sportswear, too. Athletes practising their sport can do so wearing clothes designed with a view to attractive colours and fashion. And a nice, firm tushie can look even nicer in well-cut pants.

Care: Modern fabrics are extremely wear-resistant. Frequent washing doesn't affect their functionality, form, or colour. After a wash, they dry quickly and don't absorb unpleasant smells if they're not worn several times in a row for exercising without in-between washing.

Weather: No matter whether it's hot or cold, functional sports clothes always provide the right climate for the body. In cold weather, insulating layers keep the body's temperature at a high level; in the heat, particularly lightweight fabrics feel cool on the skin.

Injuries: Wearing clothing that incorporates highly reflective fabric somewhere on it makes athletes much more visible even in twilight and the dark. This helps reduce the occurance of traffic accidents and collisions. Particularly robust fabrics don't rip in the event of a fall, minimising your risk of incurring painful abrasions.

A torch worn on the head also helps prevent injuries at twilight.

EAT AND JOG YOUR WAY TO HEALTH AND SLIMNESS

*I*n the following pages, we will take a look at your nutrition habits. The notorious "yo-yo effect" will often kick in more strongly than one could have anticipated before starting a diet. What's the reason for this? We will also discuss matters of energy balance in the context of various sports activities and different forms of exercise, including questions such as whether it's true that you burn more fat when moving as slowly as possible. You will find detailed yet easy-to-use tips for greater endurance and slimness through the right kind of diet, improving your performance in sports, work, and everyday life.

For many people, one of the major motivations for taking up running is the desire to lose weight. Looking into the energy balance of different activities is illuminating in this respect.

Energy Consumption

*Y*our energy consumption varies depending on whether you sleep, sit or stand. Obviously, it will be higher when you are in motion. Take a look at what you have to do in order to burn off the calories contained in a frozen pizza (200–250 kcal/

Rate of energy burned in various activities measured in kcal per kg body weight (per hour) and for a person weighing 70 kg.

		70kg			70kg
Sleeping	0.95	66.5	Nordic Walking/Skating	8.5	595
Sitting	1.05	73.5	Cycling (15.5 mph)	10	700
Standing	1.5	105	Jogging (7.5 mph)	10.9	763
Walking (3.5 mph)	3.2	224	Swimming (2 mph)	11.8	825
Fast Walking (4.5 mph)	5.6	392	X-country skiing (6 mph)	13.2	924

100 grams/3½ oz, depending on the toppings, or 800–1000 kcal in a typical portion of about 400 grams/14 oz) or in a bar of chocolate (100 grams/3½ oz = 600 kcal).

Your energy balance will change as soon as you start exercising and your body starts building up muscle, as this active body mass fundamentally alters your metabolism. Muscle mass is active and well-vascularised, and it consumes energy even when you're at rest, as opposed to the "dead mass" of fat tissue that you carry around with you. The morphological restructuring of your tissue has a double effect on energy consumption. Also, don't forget that even after exercising, your energy consumption rate continues to be higher for a considerable amount of time, even when you're resting. This is a result of the regenerative process, the increased blood circulation and oxygen supply to the tissues used while exercising, and the so-called afterburner effect.

Breathing is More Important than Diet

Building up more muscle mass will increase your basic rate of energy consumption even when you aren't running. Don't be surprised if at first you actually gain weight after starting your exercise program: muscles weigh more than fat tissue. However, after three to four months, your weight will have levelled off at your "competition weight". Ideally, in spite of any weight gain due to building muscle mass, this should be near your ideal weight (110 lbs plus 4 lbs for every inch over 5 feet; i.e. for 5 feet 9 inches, 110 lbs + 9 times 4 lbs = 146 lbs). If your weight was much higher than that before you started working out and you can't seem to get there, that's okay. Also, if this is the case, you shouldn't try to starve yourself until the last ounce of fat is gone. Rather, you should make sure you feel good and that you

Just going without fast food can make a huge difference...

exercise regularly. While it is true that breathing is more important than food, it's also true that deep breathing, as you do when exercising, which provides your body with more oxygen, is more important than dieting. The problem with dieting is that you're scaling down your metabolism to a lower level by cutting down on the food supply. After the diet is over and you're back to "normal" eating, however, you will put on that weight even faster. This is what is known as the yo-yo effect – it's that simple. Your metabolism cannot reach a balanced state. It needs exercise and an ongoing, high rate of energy consumption to achieve that.

Losing Weight Is a Snap ...

Sure! And you don't even have to break into a sweat! This obstinate myth was probably invented by ambitious US fitness industry gurus. It is so simple: to lose weight, you simply have to burn more calories than you take in. It is true that when you jog slowly, and the body thus has abundant oxygen, it is more inclined to switch into fat-burning mode and go easy on the carbohydrate reserves in your muscles and liver. This is a natural protective function of your body, to work as economically as possible.

The role that fat-burning plays in bodily energy production is proportional to the shape you're in: your metabolism has to learn to use fat-burning as a resource first through economisation.

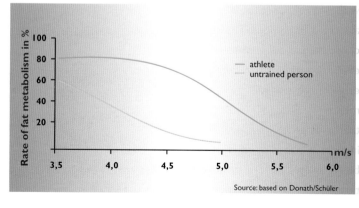

Source: based on Donath/Schüler

...But Not Through Fasting or Slow Jogging Alone

When you run at a high speed, the situation is reversed: when the demand for oxygen surpasses your oxygen intake, your body has to make carbohydrates available, which burn more quickly than fat (see the diagram below left). With increasing speed, fat burning is reduced. Obviously, you will still consume more energy at a quicker pace, if in the form of carbohydrates. Figuratively spoken, you could think of this in terms of super premium (carbohydrates) and diesel (fats) in a motor fuel context.

Basically, the longer and faster you run, the more energy you will consume. If you're jogging at a low speed, the energy demand will be correspondingly low. You have to cover quite a distance if you want to run off that piece of pizza or an ice cream sundae! Also, another aspect enters the picture when running at a higher speed: immediately following the exercise, you'll feel depleted and not hungry at all. To be sure, this is an aggressive approach to losing weight – but it's effective, too. If you have been to a gym before, you may well have seen the type of person who, leaning back and leafing through a magazine, cycles along without producing even one drop of sweat. That's exercise as an alibi: pretending to be working out, easing one's conscience, but without any real effect on your health. The effort should be a part of exercising, and it can be fun, too, especially when you're experiencing your first athletic achievements. The reading exercise on the recliner bike isn't much more than a little entertainment for the evening hours. Even shopping in running shoes or sneakers, carrying a bag in each hand, would be considerably more efficient than that – assuming that you leave the car.

Shadow boxing in front of a mirror may boost your ego, but it's doubtful if it's doing anything for your figure.

The Basics of
Healthy Nutrition

*A*ll experts agree that you're allowed to gobble up as many vegetables and fruit (with some limitations) as we can stomach. This is because they are rich in nutrients (vitamins, minerals) in proportion to their mass. Moreover, they contain a high amount of fibre, ensuring that a lot of the food is excreted as cellulose without being digested, thus contributing to weight loss.

Vegetables contain a high amount of antioxidants that protect your body from free radicals and slow down the ageing process of your cells.

Goodbye to Cell Stress!

Have you ever asked yourself why middle aged men have a much higher risk of cardiovascular disease than women in the same age group? Scientists believe that the accumulation of iron in the organism leads to cell stress. Excess iron in the bloodstream, which women are able to dispose of monthly through menstruation until they reach menopause, leads to an enzymatic reaction that produces hydroxyl radicals, the most aggressive radicals of them all. Free radicals cause and worsen existing arteriosclerosis (which can lead to heart attacks and strokes), cancer (especially of the stomach, the colon, the prostate, the lung and the breast), and other diseases of civilisation and ageing processes. This theory is supported by the fact that the risk

of cardiovascular diseases in women rises after menopause and is almost equal to that of men.

The most effective protection against cell stress is to make sure you eat plenty of vegetables that are rich in

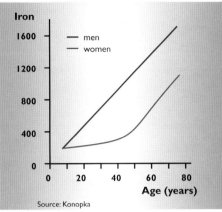

Source: Konopka

As we age, increasing amounts of iron accumulate in the body, more so in men than in women. A correlation between iron levels and cardiovascular diseases has been established.

antioxidants. Antioxidants include the vitamins C and E, as well as a number of secondary plant compounds such as beta carotene, phytosterines (contained in nuts and seeds; they inhibit cholesterol intake), saponins, glucosinolates (contained in cabbage, horseradish and mustard; they prevent cancer), flavonoids (act as immune modulators), phyto-oestrogens (contained in soy and cereals; they counter-act cancer and osteoporosis) and sulphides (contained in garlic and onions; they counter-act bacteria and actively lower blood pressure). A large number of studies have confirmed that a higher intake of vegetables and fruits correlates with a noticeably lower occurrence of cardiovascular diseases and cancer.

Take Five

It has been demonstrated that the intake of isolated dietary supplements in the form of pills or capsules does not have the same beneficial health effects as the regular consumption of fruit and vegetables. Obviously, the right combination of the ingredients is relevant for these positive effects.

For this reason, your diet should include vegetables and fruit at least five times a day: three servings of vegetables and two

portions of fruit, to be precise. One serving is approximately a handful, which amounts to 500–800 grams a day. In fact, the majority of people eat no more than 100 grams of fruit and vegetables a day (a small apple, for instance). This is clearly not enough. Why not have a delicious snack of uncooked vegetables or fruit instead of a fatty and overly sweet chocolate bar? Your health is worth it!

Certain Fats Have a Protective Function, Too

The most important components in nutritional fats are the fatty acids. Fatty acids are divided into three groups according to their chemical structure: saturated fatty acids, simple unsaturated fatty acids and multiple unsaturated fatty acids. Saturated fatty acids are mainly contained in animal fats and in fat-rich food of animal origin. However, they can also be produced as a byproduct of human metabolism itself.

Olive and rapeseed oils contain more simple unsaturated fats than other kinds of oil. Rapeseed oil contains a lot of omega-3 fatty acids, which can have an anti-inflammatory effect.

Simple Unsaturated – Doubly Good for You!

In oils of plant origin, unsaturated fatty acids outweigh other fatty acids. Simple unsaturated fatty acids – oleic acid, for instance which makes up 70 % of the fatty acids that are contained in olive oil – have low oxidation susceptibility, i. e., the single double bond in the molecule causes them to react less strongly with other substances compared to multiple unsaturated fatty acids. If a fatty acid has two or more double bonds within the carbon chain, it is referred to as a multiple unsaturated fatty acid. An example in point would be linoleic acid. The human body cannot produce multiple unsaturated acids; this is why they are called essential fatty acids, indicating that they have to be ingested with our food. They oxidise more easily, and oxidised fatty acids are harmful to

he organism, since their oxidation modifies the LDL (low density
lipoprotein) particles, which are attacked by the immune system's
own phagocytes. This leads to the generation of so-called foam
cells, which tend to attach themselves to blood vessel walls, thus
potentially leading to vascular constrictions.

By consuming more simple unsaturated fatty
acids in our diet – contained mainly in olive
oil, rapeseed oil and nuts – you gain protection against arteriosclerosis and an anti-
inflammatory effect – which, by the way,
also applies to your musculoskeletal system.
The multiple unsaturated omega-3 fatty
acids have a similar effect. They are contained in high concentration in fish oil, but
also in linseed oil, rapeseed oil and walnuts.
If you don't enjoy eating fish at all, you
can also take fish oil in the form of capsules;
they are readily available at most any super-
market.

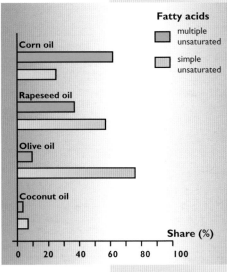

Proportion of multiple and simple unsaturated fatty acids in various kinds of oil.

What about Cholesterol?

Cholesterol has a complicated chemical formula, and it is produced exclusively in the bodies of animals and human beings.
Accordingly, it is found in all foods of animal origin, from milk
to butter and eggs as well as meat and fish. Caviar, for instance,
is a true cholesterol bomb! The greatest proportion of the
cholesterol found in the human organism, however, is made by
our own bodies. We need it as a building block for our cells, in
order to produce hormones, and as an ingredient of bile. Cholesterol, therefore, is vital – but we don't have to take it in
through foods.

Too much LDL cholesterol in our blood can be harmful to the body, and it can cause arteriosclerosis. Another type of cholesterol, on the other hand, the HDL type, helps to keep blood vessel walls elastic. Plants cannot produce cholesterol; they contain phytosterines instead (see page 43), which are similar to cholesterol and inhibit, in turn, the absorption of cholesterol in the intestines. This means that plant-based fats are naturally cholesterol-free, and they even have an anti-cholesterol effect.

Butter, a fat of animal origin, naturally contains quite a lot of cholesterol. However, as a natural product, it is preferable to processed, hardened plant fats, such as some margarines.

Meat – Yes or No?

A few words more are in order regarding the bad reputation of meat: after all, meat contains considerable amounts of selenium and zinc, important substances for immune protection. Moreover it provides a wide range of type-B vitamins and high quality proteins. Lack of an important source of nutrients, such as meat can lead to severe nutritional deficiency symptoms. It is not always possible to compensate for this lack by adding supplementary nutrients to your diet. Aim for moderation in everything, as the wise saying goes.

You can indulge in a juicy steak every once in a while.

Our recommendation: have meat once a week, and fish two times a week. And make sure you eat white meat, such as chicken, every once in a while, since it contains less iron (see page 42f). This advice applies in particular as we age.

Insider Tips from Endurance Athletes

While this book is not the place for a thorough introduction to the science of nutrition and cooking, we can nonetheless share some secrets with regard to sports nutrition that top athletes know about.

Vitamin C: Not Just for the Immune System

You're used to taking vitamin C whenever you want to protect yourself against a cold during times of increased risk. However, there's more to vitamin C, also known as ascorbic acid. It is the most important fitness and weight loss vitamin, and the glands that are in charge of producing hormones are full of it. The pituitary gland produces growth hormones, which act as natural slimming agents. The production of sex hormones, which in turn assist muscle growth, is boosted by vitamin C intake as well. Frequently, overweight people don't have enough of this miracle vitamin in their blood. This in itself is reason enough to recommend having a little fruit more often.

Citrus fruits contain a lot of vitamin C.

Beware of Excessive Carb-Loading!

Athletes' famous pasta dinners will boost your blood sugar level for a short time, only to make your body produce insulin, which will send that blood sugar level plummeting through the floor a while later. High quantities of insulin prevent your metabolism from switching into fat-burning mode. Practically speaking, this means carbo-loading is not a problem, but make sure to fill up these glycogen deposits three to five days before a marathon. Also, while running, drink carbohydrate-rich drinks to slow the depletion of your glycogen reserves. In short, avoid taking in pure carbohydrates immediately before a race or at start time.

Pasta party with a difference: paella, served at the Majorca Marathon.

Proteins – It's All about the Right Mix!

No type of food naturally contains an optimal makeup of all amino acids. For that reason, it makes sense to mix foods. A chicken egg, for instance, has a biological value of 100, while beef only makes it to 83. The combination of wheat and milk, however, has a value of 105, and the combination of potatoes and eggs tops it all with a biological protein value of 137: precisely those essential amino acids that are not present in potatoes are contained in the white of the chicken egg.

Why Magnesium Matters When Losing Weight

Just like vitamin C and iodine, magnesium is a natural slimming agent. It activates G-proteins that indirectly help the so-called "second messengers" to release fat from the cells. Magnesium is a true super-mineral that also stimulates your hormone metabolism. It can be found in anything that's green, as it is an ingredient of chlorophyll. Have some Swiss chard, spinach, Savoy cabbage or kale!

Bananas not only contain large quantities of potassium, but are also rich in magnesium

Sports and Fluid Balance

You may be aware already that 50 to 70 per cent of the human body consists of water. As we age, the proportion of water content slowly but steadily decreases: while the body of a newborn baby consists to 70 per cent of water, for example, the water content of a 50-year-old only amounts to 50 per cent. Water is extremely important for the proper functioning of our bodies: every single chemical reaction in our complex organism take place in combination with water in some way. Water is the main factor responsible for our thermoregulation. Our blood consists primarily of water, and it is necessary for processing metabolic product in the kidneys.

In sports, just a 1 or 2 per cent loss of water can already lead to a 10 per cent decrease in performance. Severe dehydration can cause cramps, nausea and shivering. For all these reasons it is highly important to ensure proper hydration during exercise, and that means you must drink before you experience thirst. Two or three hours before exercising, you should drink 300–700 ml (½ pint–1¼ pints) and up to an additional 150 ml (¼ pint) 30 minutes before. During exercise, you should drink 150–300 ml (¼–½ pint) every 15 to 20 minutes, and as much as possible following exercising in order to facilitate regeneration.

What Makes a Sports Drink?

The main purpose of hydration is to counteract the dehydration caused by sweating as quickly as possible. The absorption of liquid into the bloodstream is greatly facilitated if the drink contains sodium (400–1100 mg per litre/35 fl oz) and carbohydrates (30–80 grams per litre/35 fl oz); larger quantities, however, have an adverse effect. The intake of carbohydrates also contributes to keeping your blood sugar level in the normal range and helps keep your glycogen reserves intact. After exercising, it is a good idea to add some calcium and magnesium, as well as other minerals and trace elements, to your drink.

Drink, drink, drink… this is especially important during marathons in the heat, such as this one in Long Beach, CA.

Juice or Energy Drink?

Compared to an isotonic or sports drink, fruit juice has the disadvantage of containing organic ingredients that slow down its absorption into the bloodstream.

49

TRAINING
WITH HEART AND MIND

*D*o you like to go easy on yourself every now and then? To just jog along at the pace your legs choose, having a walking break whenever you feel like it? That's fine if you don't have a specific goal and you want to take it easy. However, even if you're running for no other reason than to benefit your health, there are some principles of exercise theory you should keep in mind.

The solitude of the long distance runner…

The Principle of Exertion and Regeneration

*T*he success of your training is based on an appropriate balance of exercise and regeneration. What is actually happening during a single training session? After all, you don't become fitter and fitter during an 8-mile endurance run – in fact, it's quite the opposite: your body grows increasingly tired, and under physical strain your performance decreases over time. Now you may ask yourself: what am I exercising for, then? Does it make any sense at all? Yes, in fact, it does: at first, the exhaustion throws your body off balance – and this is exactly what you want to happen in order for the subsequent adjustment process to take place. Think of the adjustment that occurs after physical strain and exhaustion as resulting in a kind of overreaction (this is illustrated in the figure below).

The diagram below illustrates the principle of exercise, exhaustion and over-compensation (supercompensation). If the recovery phase is too long, your body will not respond at all, because the increased performance readiness has already dropped down to its initial level again (cf. the end of the curve to the right).

The technical term for this phenomenon – restoring performance potential to a level higher than the initial one after a period of exhaustion – is "supercompensation". The whole idea behind training is to catch that upper peak of the supercompensation curve in order to get

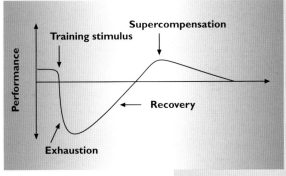

the most out of your next training session. If you manage to do this, your performance curve will soon look like this:

It is incredibly fascinating to experience this process happening to your own body, because you can actually feel the progress week after week, and you will be able to measure it based on

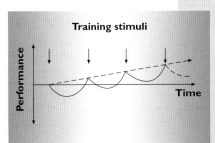

This is how your performance readiness will develop over time if you make sure to exercise only after your body has recovered.

Running addiction knows no limits, whether it's rainy winter days or highway bridges…

your speed. You will become increasingly fast, and one day, you will feel as if you're flying without any extra effort. This phenomenon may very well play a part in making you addicted to regular running.

This sense of euphoria, however, may also tempt you to overdo it, and not give your body enough time for regeneration (or any time at all, for that matter).

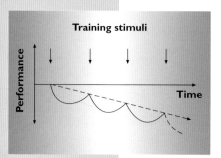

Too many training stimuli too close together lead straight to an all-time low.

If you exercise too frequently, you will never experience the joys of supercompensation – instead, you will inevitably bring yourself to an all-time low. Be sure to keep one or two days of rest in between training sessions, especially early on in your training. These restoration phases, of course, should take different forms depending on what type of training you're doing and the demands placed on your body. A long run of more than an hour that slows down toward the end, for instance, will consume more of your energy reserves (i.e. glycogen) than a shorter, faster run of about half an hour. The time required to regenerate depends on several factors, including:

- Your current level of fitness, your age and gender
- The type of food you eat directly after exercise to replenish your glycogen reserves
- How you handle the restoration phase (see the following chapter about how to speed up regeneration)
- Stresses you may be experiencing at home or at work
- Your sleeping patterns

How to Regulate Training Intensity

*E*specially if you're just starting out, don't put too much confidence in your subjective sense of physical strain. Instead, observe your heart rate. The ideal level of intensity for your first six to eight weeks, which will become the foundation for future and more intense exercise, should remain in your aerobic heart rate range. This ensures you are taking in abundant oxygen ("aerobic": occurring in the presence of oxygen; "anaerobic": occurring in the absence of oxygen). At the same time, you will burn a considerable quantity of fat in the process of your overall energy production (as explained in the preceding chapter). This level of intensity is 60 to maximally 75 per cent of your maximum heart rate (MHR). Some heart rate monitoring devices, which can be worn on the wrist just like a watch, let you input parameters such as your age, weight, sex, etc. and then compute your maximum heart rate automatically, thus sparing you a maximum-effort test.

It's easy to keep your heart rate in the desired range with a heart rate monitor worn on your wrist.

The general rule of thumb for calculating your maximum heart rate (MHR) is as follows:

MHR (men) = 220 minus age

MHR (women) = 226 minus age

For example, for a 44-year-old female: MHR = 226 minus 44, or 182. Your optimal initial training heart rate is 60 to 75 per cent of 182 – at this rate, the generous supply of oxygen ensures low lactate values (clearly within the aerobic range) even while burning fat – specifically, that is 110–140 heart beats per minute. This is in line with the diagram on the next page.

You will find various formulae for determining maximum HR in books. Sometimes, only half or three quarters of one's age are subtracted from 220. We prefer to stay on the safe side, assuming

the full age, which leads to a lower heart rate. This way, you will not over-exercise. A person with a higher resting pulse will have a higher MHR, and it's a fact that your MHR decreases with age.

The only way to objectively determine your individual MHR, however, is to perform a maximum-effort test. This can be done in various ways. As a beginner, you should only take a maximum-effort test under medical supervision, including an ECG check, if possible while running on a treadmill with progressive increases

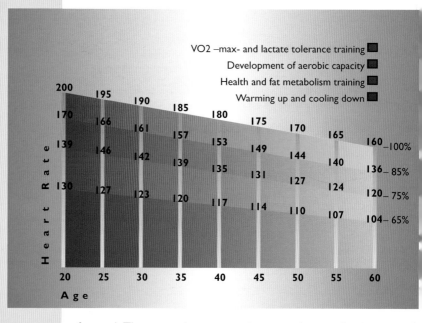

This diagram illustrates the relationship between heart rate and age.

of speed. The exact heart rate, however, is not the important thing in easy, aerobic training: you should stay within that range of 60 to 75 per cent of your MHR in order to get fit. These heart rates should only be considered guideline values. Your pulse rate may be influenced by a number of factors, such as recent illness, and there are people who simply naturally have higher and lower resting heart rates. If you want to know for sure, consider taking a lactate test. This test determines the amount of lactate in your

bloodstream at various levels of exertion and makes it possible to specifically determine your own personal aerobic threshold heart rate. The method is objective and only involves taking a few drops of blood from your earlobe. Until quite recently, this method for assessing training intensity was only available to top athletes; these days it is increasingly available for amateur athletes, as well. Everyone can determine their ideal aerobic training threshold.

Ouch! Don't worry, you'll hardly feel the little sting in your earlobe. This picture shows an athlete undergoing a lactate test after a race in order to determine her body's recovery patterns. The method used is the same as the service available to you at special institutes, where you can have your lactate performance curve analysed while running on a treadmill.

After that, you can assess your heart rate in a more precise manner, so you'll have a reference point for your training in the weeks and months to come, constantly monitored by a heart rate monitor worn on your wrist.

If you shouldn't own a heart rate monitor yet, just stop running for 15 seconds and touch your carotid artery with your thumb and index finger for about 10 seconds – your pulse should be easily palpable. Multiply your count by six. Do not count for longer than 10 to 15 seconds, because your heart rate might have already slowed down by the end of a longer interval – especially if you tend to regenerate quickly – which can distort the results. You have to keep in mind that top athletes are able to regenerate within one minute, to the point where they're ready for the next training interval. In other words, this means that your heart rate may drop by 30 to 40 beats within that time span, e.g. from 180 to 146.

The lactate curve of this amateur runner indicates that his aerobic/anaerobic threshold is somewhere near 15 km/hour (9 mph) or 4 minutes/km (6.4 minutes/mile). Theoretically, and under different circumstances (after preparing the muscles for a marathon distance) this would enable him to run a marathon in about 2:50.

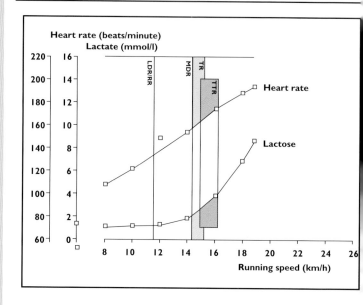

Factors that Determine How Hard Your Body Works

Running Speed (Intensity)

Frequently, the running speed during normal continuous running is much too high. Your speed should correspond to a lactate value of 1-2 mmol lactate/dl of blood. This can be thoroughly tested through a lactate test (see the list of selected institutions on page 95) and adapted to your active heart rate, which can be comfortably checked with a heart rate monitor during exercise. The corresponding performance level is 65 to 75 per cent of your maximum heart rate; this also is the performance area in which more fats than carbohydrates are burned as fuel, relative to the overall energy consumption. Certain women's magazines sometimes – unprofessionally – refer to this as a fat-melting process; however, with increasing intensity, a greater amount of energy overall is burned. Our advice: you should be able to carry on a conversation while running, even about sophisticated matters, without undue effort. Run at the speed and for the length of time that keep you on a level that leaves you in a comfortable state when you finish exercising, so that your legs don't feel heavy. If you stick to this rule, you ensure that you will be able to look forward to your training the next day, and that you will enjoy it and feel as fresh as a daisy all over again.

Running Course

Another important factor in controlling exercise intensity is your running course. Not only will ascents and descents inevitably cause variation in running speed, your body also has to adopt in terms of its position. This way, different muscles are exercised. Your exercise will inevitably turn into an interval exercise based on the terrain. On descents, you will be able to regenerate; or, rather, your circulation will, because descents can be a high strain on your muscles. On ascents, make sure you don't breathe too heavily. Shift gears as required to ensure that your metabolism does not switch into anaerobic mode, which is less beneficial to your health.

Dune runs are the hardest method for increasing exercise intensity through choice of running course and should only be attempted by top runners. These runs have a double intensity-increasing effect: the soft sand and the ascent.

Course Length or Duration of Exercise (Volume)

A widespread and mistaken belief is that performance increase in long-distance running can only be achieved by increasing the distance. While it is true that a certain number of miles a week is necessary for running a marathon, your actual performance depends on the quality of the training. Two factors are especially important: your maximum speed, e.g. your three- or six-mile record, on the one hand, and your metabolism's potential on the other, i.e., how long you're able to keep up high speed. Two types of exercise are important in this context: fartlek training in varied terrain, with varying blocks of intensity (e.g. 3-5-4-3-2 minutes with five-minute breaks in between during which you jog along at

an easy speed and recover), or threshold tempo runs (as described in the following section on your full-year training program).

The more frequently you run, the more often you should vary your route.

Training Frequency and Intensity

Usually, people refer to the frequency of training sessions per week when they talk about training schedules. However, sometimes, frequency refers to units within one exercise session (e.g. in the case of interval exercises such as 12 x 400 metres). As mentioned above, for the purpose of fitness sports, you should get exercise for at least 20 to 30 minutes three or four times a week, otherwise you will not achieve many positive effects for your health. Take another look at the diagram illustrating exercise and regeneration. In interval training, a crucial factor for the frequency is the duration and type of rest intervals, which, in turn, affect the overall intensity of the training. The length of the rest intervals depends on other factors, such as speed (intensity), distance (duration) and your ability to regenerate (i.e. your athletic condition).

How to Plan Your Training Year

Always divide your individual full-year training schedule, or your four- or six-month training schedule in preparation for a race, into three phases. This principle is taken from competitive sports, where athletes exercise for two preparation periods (general and special) and one or two competition periods (including an in-between maintenance period if there are several

competitions), and a subsequent transition period used for active relaxation. So, strictly spoken, it's four phases. What matters to you are the preparation periods. For the purpose of fitness sports, we will divide the preparation period into an adjustment period, a build-up period, and a stabilisation period.

Recommendations for Organising Training Periods

Assuming that you will take part in two to four running events a year, a training program that takes into account the seasons could look like this: start training late in autumn, do alternative endurance sports. Try to slowly accustom your musculoskeletal system to the strain of running. Start out with a maximum of 50 per cent of the target distance of your overall program. If the weather is bad, use an exercise bike at home or at the gym. Use any type of cardio machine you enjoy.

Variation throughout the Year

If you don't like gyms, try cross-country skiing – it's the best substitute for running as far as exercise goes. Make sure to at least try it during your winter vacation. Compared to running, your heart rate gets an extra boost from the additional exercise of your arms and from the altitude. In February and March, begin systematic threshold training. Schedule a fartlek run or some long interval tempo runs (e.g., a 1 mile run at your half-marathon speed, five to eight times) once a week. Be sure to keep your speed at a level that would allow you to run more rounds than those you've scheduled. During tempo runs keep telling yourself: "Take it easy, quantity makes the difference in the end". Even after six to eight rounds, you should still feel like you could add two or three more. Threshold training focuses on improving your performance in the 2–4 mmol lactate range, meaning that you should stay just below the anaerobic range, just before you start panting. After all, you're not trying to become a middle distance runner who has to build up buffer substances in order to better tolerate high levels of lactic acid. Moreover, excessive lactate production

is damaging to your aerobic system, your cell membranes and more. It has only very little to do with fitness training.

For pacing runs, you should choose a measured track. Use a heart rate monitor and find a training buddy, too.

If you're planning to run your first marathon in autumn, sign up for your first fun races around the end of March or the beginning of April, about 10K and then a half-marathon two or three weeks later. After your first two racing experiences, shift gears again and relax a little. This way you'll be able to take up your training program to the full extent early in summer, the most beautiful season. As a beginner, by now you should be running 25 to 35 miles (40–55 km) a week.

If you choose this type of long term build-up training, you will have nothing to worry about when the day of your debut arrives.

Planning Is Half the Battle

In two months, I will run six miles. One month later, I'll do a half-marathon, three months after that, my first marathon... As a beginner, this kind of pressure is guaranteed to ruin the fun experience of running for you – instead, injuries and overtraining are bound to happen.

We don't believe that every leisure-time runner and every beginner has to be drilled to run a marathon distance; if, however, you should set this goal for yourself, make sure to approach it in a reasonable fashion. Make time for it – at least a year. Learn about your training forms first.

The Main Forms of Training for Health and Fitness

Endurance Runs

Endurance running is the basic training form for both amateur and professional runners.

In practice, we distinguish three forms:

LR – long recovery run at 65–75% of your MHR

MLR – medium long run at 75–85% of your MHR

TR – tempo or threshold run at 85–90% of your MHR

Depending on the training phase you're in, the ratio between these three should be 60% (LR) to 30% (MLR) to 10% (TR or threshold tempo run, see below).

Assuming that you're a beginning marathon runner with a four-hour target, and that you run 30 miles per week after a half year of training, that amounts to:

30 km/18 miles (LR) (1–1.5 mmol lactate)

15 km/9 miles (MLR) (1.5–2.5 mmol lactate)

5 km/3 miles (TR) (2.5–4 mmol lactate)

Be sure to balance the values above with the age-heart rate diagram on page 54, especially if you're not planning to get a professional lactate test to determine your current performance. If, on the other hand, you take such a test, you will be well in-formed about your target values for each training form.

Fartlek

Fartlek is an odd-sounding word that means "speed play" in Swedish, and that's just what it is. In fartlek training, you can either adjust your speed to the terrain or other landmarks as you see fit; or you follow a predetermined, timed pattern of short- and medium-long intense stretches, all under 10 minutes (e.g. 3-5-6-4-2). These fast stretches should be run at threshold speed, while in between you should jog at an easy pace to recover, at least as long as the preceding fast spurt.

Tempo Runs (Threshold)

Tempo runs are primarily intended to improve your oxygen intake capacity. You shouldn't be at much higher than 90 per cent of your MHR. Expressed in mmol lactate you want to be in the range of 3 to max. 5 mmol, i.e., the aerobic-anaerobic threshold. Typical short-interval programs are 15 times 300 metres or 10 to 12 times 400 metres. Depending on which training phase you are in, you should run them at your 5K or 10K (3- or 6-mile) pace, obviously starting out with the slower.

With regard to long intervals, 8 to 10 intervals of 1000 metres have proven to be effective when training for a marathon or half-marathon. As you get started, extend these to 4 to 5 x 2000 metres at your marathon pace, then after 4 to 8 weeks of training progress to 3 to 4 x 3000 metres . Once you have done that pick up the 1000-metres intervals again, this time at your half-marathon pace. This increases the intensity of your training sessions; then you can go on and increase the distance at the quicker pace as described above.

Running Hills

Ascents and descents force you to adjust your pace to the terrain. Especially in hilly regions, they can hardly be avoided. When running uphill you should shorten your stride, run with a stronger push-off and swing your arms. The upper body should lean forward slightly. To train this skill, focus on muscular endurance. Suitable forms include fartlek or threshold tempo runs. The latter, however, should only be attempted by advanced runners because of the challenging nature of the terrain. Organise your workout in short intervals as described above.

For hill running, an asphalt street is sometimes preferable to gravel tracks, which involve a higher risk of slipping and injuries.

Crescendo Running

This is the preferred form of endurance running among Kenya's top athletes: you start out very easy and then gradually accel-

erate, slowly "rolling" your fat metabolism into higher speed. This has the huge advantage that's also important in a race situation: from the start you save your glycogen reserves, which you're going to need for the quick pace toward the end. This is why it is so important to start out cautiously and reasonably in a race. Just take the first half more slowly than the second one.

Given this knowledge and the following table, you can easily organise a training schedule that will increase your stamina:

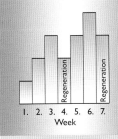

Sample Weeks for Half-Marathons and Marathons
for 3:30- to 4-hour runners
50–70 km/30–43 miles, 3–5 workouts per week,
6–8 hours per week

Adjustment period

Mo –

Tu 10 km/6 mile endurance run (LR), strength endurance training (endurance exercises as described on pages 68–71)

We (Optional if goal is 4 hours) 15–16 km/9–10 mile LR

Th 10–11 km/6–7 mile NLR, stretching, several 100-m acceleration sprints

Fr –

Sa (Optional) alternative workout (for example, aqua jogging, Nordic Walking, cycling, swimming)

Su Long jog (80–100 minutes)

Build-up period

Mo 10–12 km/6–7.5 mile LR

Tu –

We Week 1: 10 min WUR/CDR, 10 km/6 mile TR (see above);
Week 2: 10–15 min WUR/CDR, 6–8 x 1000 m at marathon pace, 3-minute threshold run;
Week 3: WUR/CDR, 12–15 x 300 m (5K and 10K pace)
In the following weeks, increase intensity as described above (first the length, then the speed) until you can comfortably run about 4 x 3000 metres at your half-marathon pace. This will probably take 4 to 5 months.

Th Alternative training (60 minutes), strength workout

Fr –

Sa 10–15 km/6–9 mile LR

Su Long jog, 2–2½ hours or at least 3 hours of a different sport; in a long jog, you slowly approach your maximum intensity, increasing duration up to 3½ hours. Keep in mind that you don't have to keep going at your marathon speed – it's the length of time that matters!
Fartlek training every other week, 10 min WUR/CDR, 6–10–6–4–2 minute intervals running at half-marathon pace or 15–18 km/9–11 mile tempo run, progressively increasing.

The principle of progressive build-up consists in increasing the amount of training for about three weeks followed by a regeneration period, and then another build-up period that starts at a higher level. Do not increase your training by more than 10 per cent within a week.

3:30:00		4:00:00	
1 km	0:04:59	1 km	0:05:41
2 km	0:09:57	2 km	0:11:23
3 km	0:14:56	3 km	0:17:04
4 km	0:19:54	4 km	0:22:45
5 km	0:24:53	5 km	0:28:26
6 km	0:29:52	6 km	0:34:08
7 km	0:34:50	7 km	0:39:49
8 km	0:39:49	8 km	0:45:30
9 km	0:44:48	9 km	0:51:11
10 km	0:49:46	10 km	0:56:53
11 km	0:54:45	11 km	1:02:34
12 km	0:59:43	12 km	1:08:15
13 km	1:04:42	13 km	1:13:57
14 km	1:09:41	14 km	1:19:38
15 km	1:14:39	15 km	1:25:19
16 km	1:19:38	16 km	1:31:00
17 km	1:24:36	17 km	1:36:42
18 km	1:29:35	18 km	1:42:23
19 km	1:34:34	19 km	1:48:04
20 km	1:39:32	20 km	1:53:45
21 km	1:44:31	21 km	1:59:27
22 km	1:49:29	22 km	2:05:08
23 km	1:54:28	23 km	2:10:49
24 km	1:59:27	24 km	2:16:31
25 km	2:04:25	25 km	2:22:12
26 km	2:09:24	26 km	2:27:53
27 km	2:14:23	27 km	2:33:34
28 km	2:19:21	28 km	2:39:16
29 km	2:24:20	29 km	2:44:57
30 km	2:29:18	30 km	2:50:38
31 km	2:34:17	31 km	2:56:19
32 km	2:39:16	32 km	3:02:01
33 km	2:44:14	33 km	3:07:42
34 km	2:49:13	34 km	3:13:23
35 km	2:54:11	35 km	3:19:05
36 km	2:59:10	36 km	3:24:46
37 km	3:04:09	37 km	3:30:27
38 km	3:09:07	38 km	3:36:08
39 km	3:14:06	39 km	3:41:50
40 km	3:19:05	40 km	3:47:31
41 km	3:24:03	41 km	3:53:12
42 km	3:29:02	42 km	3:58:53
42,195 km	3:30:00	42,195 km	4:00:00

Km split table for total marathon times of 3:30 and 4 hours (1 km = 0.6 miles 10 km = ca. 6 miles)

Training Leading up to a Race
4–5 weeks before participating in a marathon

Mo 15 km/9 mile LR, crescendo run on the last 5 km/3 miles to 10K pace
Tu –
We WUR/CDR, strength training, acceleration runs, stretching
Th 10 km/6 mile NLR
Fr –
Sa 6–8 km/3.5–5 mile easy jog
Su 100–120 min or 10 km/6 mile fun race, or half marathon, but only up until 3 weeks before the marathon

If your aim is simply to finish, your exercise program should look similar in principle, but 3–4 sessions a week are enough. Toward the end of your training schedule, it's important to actually do the long 3- to 4-hour runs!

LR = long run, NLR = normal long run, TR = tempo run,
WUP = warm-up run, CDR = cool-down run

Additional Tips on Marathon Training

In preparing to run a marathon, distance always has priority over intensity. The challenge lies not in your speed, but in the distance to be covered.

The Last Week before the Race

No more long runs (at most one hour of easy running)! Toward the end of each workout, do 2 or 3 tempo or acceleration runs. Mentally prepare for the marathon (imagine yourself crossing the finish, positive reinforcement). Be sure to eat well and increase your fluid intake several days before the race (see the preceding chapter).

Also, look for announcements by the organisers. Most organisers will provide you with brochures with the registration forms.

This is What You Can Achieve

5 km/3 mile time x 9.8 = realistic marathon time
    Example: 19.5 minutes x 9.8 = approximately 3:11

10 km/6 mile time x 4.7 = realistic marathon time
    Example: 44 minutes x 4.7 = approximately 3:25

Speeding Up Recovery

*F*or quicker recovery after demanding running sessions, follow these pointers:

- Cool down by running slowly the last 10–15 minutes, or simply go easy for the last mile or so
- Do 10 minutes of stretching exercises
- After showering, spray your legs with cold water for a long time
- Even such a seemingly trivial thing as putting your feet up for 10 minutes makes a difference
- After that, a little 5 to 10 minute self-massage of the thighs and calf muscles

One or two days per week should be free of training, but devoted intentionally to active recuperating. Especially beneficial for this are the alternative sports described on pages 89ff, but also sauna, massage, a Jacuzzi bath, etc.

Anything beyond that requires the luxury of more time. These days it seems that few of us have the time for a yoga class twice a week. On the other hand, as soon as you've learned the exercises and positions, you could of course do a yoga program at home – if it really helps you to relax. However, we know from experience that endurance athletes have their own intrinsic vegetative relaxation system that often makes additional techniques such as autogenous training and yoga seem superfluous. The main point is, if it work for you, go right ahead and do it.

Anyone Can Jog – But What About Running?

*R*unning is the archetypal form of human movement and something we're all familiar with. Anyone who is healthy and has a functional musculoskeletal system can go ahead and start running. And every runner will develop their very own, unmistakably individual running style. A person's posture and running style mirror their body language and relationship with their body.

We naturally run in a way that feels good to us. But all individuality aside, there are some ground rules and principles regarding what an ideal running posture looks like (see the following box). We take our bearings from the natural, undistorted movement patterns we would find when running on natural soil. When running barefoot on grass or sand, our bodies' shock absorbance and cushioning mechanisms, our muscles, sinews and joints, are all employed, and impact forces are smoothly distributed. We naturally land on the middle of the foot or on the forefoot, which is why this running style is referred to as "forefoot running".

Forefoot Strikers and Heel Strikers – Variation Is Good for You

As opposed to forefoot runners, heel strikers land on their heels, which means that the shock of impact is transferred throughout the body with little absorbance. Still, there are many heel strikers who do not experience any physical problems. If that is the case for you, you don't have to change your running style. Try to

alternate between forefoot running and heel running regularly. Whether you're a forefoot- or a heel striker, there's always potential for improving and optimising your technique. It is generally recommendable to keep your runs as varied as possible and to adapt your running style based on the terrain (structure) as well as the distance (fatigue factor) of a run.

The "Optimal" Running Stance

Head: Your head should rest upright on your shoulders, as relaxed as possible. Look straight ahead.

Shoulders: Don't hunch your shoulders, but keep them loose and relaxed.

Arm position: Keep your lower and upper arms roughly at a right angle to each other, also while in motion. Swing your arms at your sides as you run.

Hands: The hands are slightly opened, the fingers relaxed. Don't make a fist or extend your fingers.

Trunk: Your upper torso stabilises the entire running gait. It should lean forward slightly, but in an upright position. Try to avoid arching your back.

Hips/legs: Your stride should be fluid, but not too long. Fully extend your knees and hips as you push off the ground. Your hips should be forward and below your centre of gravity.

Feet: Your foot should strike slightly in front of your body axis. As far as striking goes, nearly any foot position is possible and most are common (heel strike, midfoot, forefoot). This depends on your running style.

Centre of gravity: Your centre of gravity is in front of the hips and moves up and down slightly, but it should be kept as high as possible. (Try to not let your hip sink during the strike phase.)

Speed through Strength

Muscle Strength in the Appropriate Places is Crucial in Running

While the typical extremely slim serious runner doesn't exactly look like a mountain of muscle, strong muscles in the right places are in fact extremely important in running. Well-developed muscles in the torso stabilise the pelvis and help drive the body forward consistently. Weak trunk muscles, on the other hand, lead to compensating movements to the side, momentum is lost, and speed decreases. Without a strong corset of muscles, it is impossible to consistently keep your centre of gravity up high.

These strengthening exercises can be done at home. Devoting just 20 minutes to them two times a week will help guard against injuries and give you a solid basis for running faster.

Trunk strength, on your side
Extend your body and rest on your lower arm. Keep your body relaxed. Lower trunk toward floor and lift again. Variation: Lift upper leg sideways.

Leg and trunk muscles
Lie on your back, with your legs extended, resting on your lower arms. Look up. Variation: Lift one leg while keeping the body extended.

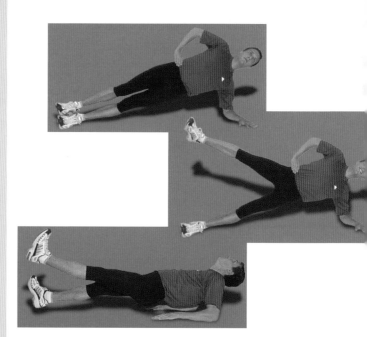

Trunk and leg strength
Propped on elbows, body extended. Look down; hold. Variation: Bend one knee and extend the other; lift the extended leg. Body is fully extended at all times.

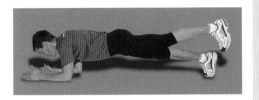

Trunk and back muscles
Kneel with your hands on the floor. Lift your left arm and left leg and fully extend them. Hold the position for about 5 seconds, then repeat with the right side.

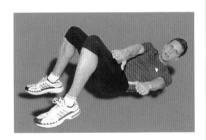

Stomach muscles
Lie on your back, knees bent, hands behind your neck. Pull the upper torso and head toward the knees. Variation: With your arms, pull diagonally toward your feet.

Strength Workout in Your Living Room

- Repeat each exercise 8–12 times (= 1 set). Do all exercises on both sides; movements should be made slowly.
- Do 2–3 sets of each exercise.
- Take short breaks in between sets (20–30 seconds), or skip rope in between.
- As soon as it's no longer possible to do an exercise properly, the set should be stopped.
- Go through the whole exercise program at least twice a week (about 20 minutes per program).

Upper back muscles and trunk stabilisation (rowing)
Sit with your legs almost fully extended. Wrap band securely around both feet and pull it with your hands so it's taut. Hold arms next to your body and pull elbows backward, maintaining a 90° angle between lower and upper arms, while actively contracting shoulder blades. Don't hunch your shoulders.

Shoulder, arm and back muscles (cross-country skiing)
Attach the middle of the band at a height above your head, e.g. on an upper doorjamb. Feet in slight stride position, centre of gravity between your legs. Contract abdominal and buttock muscles. Keep your back straight and your upper body extended and facing forward (don't lean to one side). Pull band ends from a position in front of your body down and back, at a diagonal angle. Avoid arching your back.

Shoulder rotators
Arms to the sides, bent 90°. Tightly wrap the band around both hands. Your fingertips should point forward, thumbs up. Contract abdominal muscles. Now, move both lower arms outward at the same time.

Full-body strengthening

Place both feet on the band, about in the centre, and shoulder width apart. Knees are slightly bent. Cross the ends of the band, wrap them around each your hands so that it pulls gently inward. With your palms facing away from you, move both arms simultaneously and slowly upward. Hold briefly, then slowly lower again.

Abductors (outer thighs)

Fasten both ends of the band with a knot 10-20 inches above a lower doorjamb. Place the loop around the top of the right ankle joint. Your weight rests on the left leg, which stands in front of the band. Contract abdominal and buttock muscles, feel and support the abdomen and bottom with your hands. Maintain erect posture. Slowly move your right leg outward. Hold the tension, then release. Repeat several times. All the force should come from the outer thigh and hip. Repeat with other leg.

Adductors (inner thighs)

Fasten band at lower doorjamb as described in the abductor exercise above. This time, step into the loop with your left leg. Your weight rests on the right leg. Again, contract abdominal and buttock muscles. Slowly move your left leg in toward the supporting leg. After repeating 10-15 times, switch legs again.

For Greater Flexibility

Stretching Belongs in the Repertoire of Every Athlete

*S*tretching is a way to care for our aching muscles while relaxing them at the same time. Moreover, stretching provides moments of serenity, moments of attuning to our bodies' "inner voice", and it improves our awareness and perception of our bodies. Stretching exercises can be performed to warm up, cool down, for recovery after an injury, and for regeneration. Basically, we distinguish two types of stretching.

Hip flexors
In a kneeling position, place one foot in front of you. Contract your bottom and push the same hip forward until the knee is aligned with the heel.

Static Stretching

Static stretching exercises involve holding one position. Adopt a position in which you feel tension – but not pain – in the muscle (hold 30–60 seconds). Static stretching can be done anywhere, anytime (after training, during a break at work, on the bus, at home, etc.). Along with cool-down runs, static stretching brings your muscle tension back to normal. That makes static stretching good for relaxing, but not as preparation for high-intensity exercise (intense training, competitions).

Muscles at back of thigh
Extend one leg in front of you. The extended upper body leans toward the foot, which is placed on the floor and relaxed. Hands rest on upper leg.

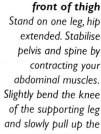

Muscles at front of thigh
Stand on one leg, hip extended. Stabilise pelvis and spine by contracting your abdominal muscles. Slightly bend the knee of the supporting leg and slowly pull up the opposite heel toward your bottom. Support yourself against a wall or a partner.

Dynamic Stretching

A good warm-up exercise aims at preparing you for the actual exercise, both mentally and physically, and brings muscle tension to an optimal level. Therefore, if you are planning quick, vigorous training then dynamic stretching is the best preparation for it. In dynamic stretching, you begin by bringing the muscle into a position in which you feel a light strain. Holding that position, you then perform small, gentle swinging movements 5–10 times. By the way: traditional gymnastics exercises are also an ideal way to warm up.

Back
Stand with your legs hips' width apart and rest your palms on your knees. First round your back, then change into an arched back. Your head should follow the motion. Repeat 5–6 times.

Calves
Point your toes down as hard as you can for about 4 seconds, then pull the toes up toward your shin as hard as you can. Repeat 2–3 times.

Spine
Start out in a straddle position. Rest your hands on your shoulders. Slowly turn trunk from one side to the other, keeping elbows at shoulders' height, and looking straight ahead. Repeat 5–6 times, turning to both sides.

73

Solidly Grounded

*R*unning with weak feet is just like cycling with flat tires! It makes good sense to invest some time and effort into your feet.

Especially for runners, strong feet are a prerequisite for being able to run fast with minimal risk of injuries. However, strong feet aren't going to appear from nowhere – you have to do something in order to get them. In our present-day industrial society, feet are only rarely used anymore to do what they have been designed to do by evolution: running barefoot. Most of the time, our feet are stuck in shoes, in softly cushioned and supportive shoes, at that.

In Kenya, you still see a lot of barefoot runners who even run races barefoot.

These shoes do all the work for us and, in the long run, muscles in our feet actually atrophy. Today, natural soil that is suitable for barefoot running can often only be found in the form of fenced-off meadows or beaches, when we're away on holiday. You have already read about the foot's natural shock-absorbing function in the chapter on anatomical basics (see pages 25ff). On the following pages we will show you how to strengthen your feet through barefoot running and simple exercises. If you exercise your feet, you will likely not have any need for sturdy pronation supports or innumerable cushioning supports in your running shoes.

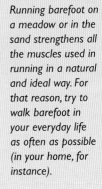

Running barefoot on a meadow or in the sand strengthens all the muscles used in running in a natural and ideal way. For that reason, try to walk barefoot in your everyday life as often as possible (in your home, for instance).

Foot exercises allow you to strengthen muscles that are rarely used in our everyday lives, and therefore tend to atrophy. The simple exercises below, performed regularly, will give the muscles in your feet extra flexibility and power.

1st starting position
Lying or sitting
Pull outer foot upward, then move soles together.
Repeat 15 times, pause.
2–3 sets.

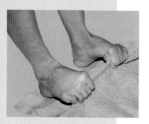

2nd starting position
Sitting
Grab onto a cloth with your toes, pull toward you or push away.
Repeat 5 times, 30-second pause.
1-2 sets.

3rd starting position
Standing
Roll up a towel and walk along it. The longitudinal arch of your foot should not bend. Maintain a straight leg axis.
Repeat 5–10 times.

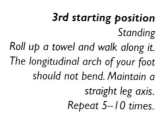

In skipping rope *you land on the forefoot, so the body's weight is absorbed by the muscles of the foot and calf.*

4th starting position
Stand on your toes on the edge of a step (e.g., a stair). Press your heel down as far as you can, then push up to stand on the tip of your toes.
Repeat 15 times, 30-second pause, 2–3 sets.

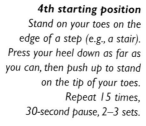
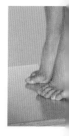
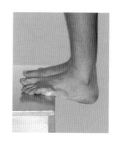

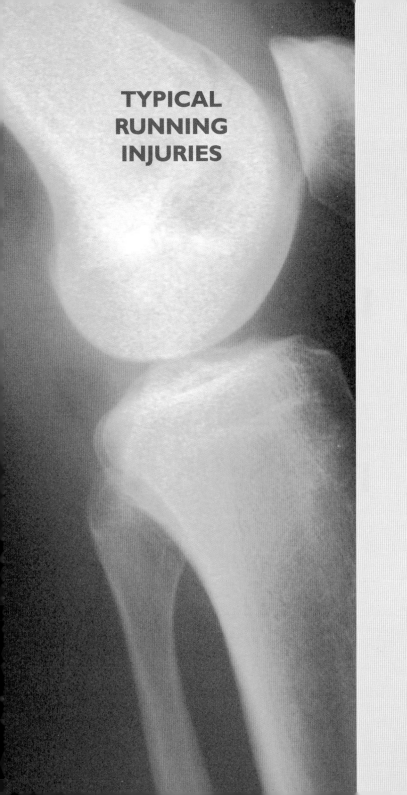

TYPICAL RUNNING INJURIES

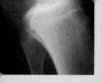

Orthopaedic Aspects of Running

by Dr. Jens Enneper

Jens Enneper, M.D., orthopaedic specialist, medical superintendent of the Cologne, Germany Ford Marathon, associated doctor of the German Athletics Association.

*F*rom an orthopaedic point of view, most problems related to running are chronic overuse injuries of the musculo-skeletal system. Compared to other sports, such as soccer or skiing, acute injuries are significantly less common. Most of the time, typical runners' injuries develop gradually and over a long period of time. They are frequently played down and, as the disease takes its course, may lead to chronic pain symptoms. The areas most frequently affected are the lower extremities. Symptoms may include pain in the knee area, the tendons and tendon sheaths and in the periosteum, but also fatigue fractures. Moreover, the number of spinal problems observed has been increasing in recent times. In the event of an injury, the first thing to be done is to locate and eliminate the cause, followed by systematic therapy.

More important than any therapy, however, is prevention. Relevant deficiencies of the musculoskeletal system can be diagnosed in a thorough sports orthopaedic check-up even before you start with a training program. This way, the risk of running injuries can be lowered.

Preventing Overuse Injuries

With each step a runner takes, the impact shock is three to four times their body weight, i. e., 460 to 620 lbs per stride for a 155-lb runner. Given this high level of stress, it is important to have the condition of your musculoskeletal system analysed by an orthopaedic specialist before beginning a training program. Such an examination includes assessments of the body's tructure including the shape of the spine and pelvis, and any otential muscular imbalance. The joints are examined with egard to their flexibility and stability, and they are checked for ny medical disorders. The results of this examination provide mportant information regarding injury prevention (on how to ectify a muscular imbalance, for instance).

deally, this static examination should be complemented by an dditional examination of the body in motion in order to losely examine the legs' axis stability and the foot's rolling attern, both with and without shoes. Over-pronation or over-upination can be recognized and counteracted at an early tage. Ignoring abnormal stress patterns over a long period of ime can lead to overuse injuries such as pain in the knees and eet or irritations of the Achilles tendon or the bursae (in the nees and hips).

People who have conditions such as bow legs or knock-knees should not run all their training miles on asphalt. In particular, they should be cautious when increasing the intensity of their training.

Apart from orthopaedic measures, the most important factor n preventing injuries is sensible training. Numerous studies ave shown that an abrupt increase of miles run weekly fre-quently leads to overuse injuries. It has been proven that the

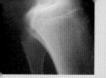

cardiovascular system is much quicker to respond and adapt to exercise than the muscles. For this reason, runners with well-trained cardiovascular systems can easily overestimate the abilities of their musculoskeletal system. Typical runners' injuries frequently occur either early on in the training or after two to three years.

Running Injuries

*I*njuries of the musculoskeletal system can be caused by an intense, one-time impact (macrotrauma) or by smaller, repeated impacts (microtrauma). Forceful impacts are relatively uncommon when it comes to running. More typically, runners have to deal with overuse injuries that result from microtrauma that occur over and over again.

If you are prone to injuries of the ankles, Achilles tendon and the knees, you should avoid gravel and loose ground, since they require extraordinary concentration and stability of the joints.

Common Acute Running Injuries

1. Ankle Sprain (Distortion)

*D*istortions of the foot are among the most common of all sports injuries. Although they are relatively rare in running, an ankle can nonetheless quickly be twisted, for instance when the layout of the course for a big running event is hardly visible and you step on a kerb. This type of injury can also take place on wet or slippery ground in autumn or winter. Partially or completely torn ligaments can result, depending on the severity of the injury. Rarely, the joint itself may suffer damage (e.g. the cartilage). Most athletes experience pain related to bearing weight on the joint, and swelling in the outer ankle area. A physician will first assess the severity of the injury and then treat it accordingly.

2. Acute Muscle Injuries

Among the acute muscle injuries that befall runners are muscle bruises, contusions, strained muscles and even muscle ruptures. In running, not surprisingly, the most common injuries are those to the lower extremities. The muscles at the back of the thighs and the calf muscles are involved particularly often.

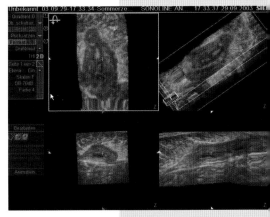

Muscle injuries are divided into three categories according to their severity:

Level I: Slight strain

Only a few muscle fibres have been torn, and the functionality of the muscle is only slightly limited. The patient might experience slight swelling and pain that correlates with movement of the muscle. Slight strains often occur in conjunction with muscle induration, or hardening of the muscle.

New imaging techniques facilitate medical diagnosis. This image shows a three-dimensional ultrasound image that makes several layers of the muscle visible.

Level II: Severe strain

This means significant damage of the muscle, but not a complete tear. Muscle functionality is considerably limited.

Level III: Muscle rupture

Severe damage of muscle, complete rupture and loss of functionality. Further injury criteria include haemorrhages (haematoma) within the muscle and injuries to the fascia that surrounds the muscle. A detailed patient interview and an in-depth examination are essential to the diagnosis of muscle injuries. Machine-aided diagnostic methods, including ultrasound and/or MRI, help confirm initial findings and in assessing the severity of the muscle injury.

3. Tendon Rupture (e.g. the Achilles tendon)

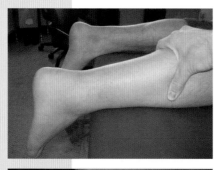

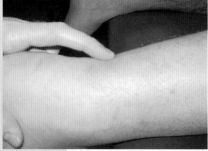

Achilles tendons with a pre-existing defect may tear partially or completely. Occasionally, a loud popping sound is reported when an Achilles tendon rupture occurs, but most often athletes experience pain in their calf when moving, along with a corresponding loss in functionality of the calf muscle. Clinically, a distinct dent can be observed in the area where the rupture occurred. Another indicator is the fact that the foot no longer flexes when the calf muscle is tensed. This method of diagnosis is called Thompson's test.

Thompson's test is a method for determining whether an Achilles tendon is completely torn. If it is, the heel and foot do not flex when the calf is tensed (top picture).

A distinct dent can be felt in the area of the rupture (bottom).

Acute Treatment Measures

The time-tested initial treatment for acute injuries follows the RICE schema (R = rest, I = ice, C = compression, E = elevation). The therapeutic goals are the alleviation of pain, prevention or reduction of swelling, and recovery of functionality. The specific therapy measures should be established by a physician. In the event of acute muscle injuries, massage should not be administered immediately. In rare cases, they can be given 72 hours after an injury occurs. Both physical and physiotherapeutic therapies can be applied. A mild compression of the injured area (with tape, an adhesive bandage or possibly neoprene stockings) can help support the injury and alleviate discomfort.

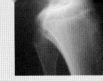

Common Overuse Injuries in Runners

I. Knee Pain

The most frequent area in which runners experience pain caused by overuse, perhaps not surprisingly, is the region of the knee joint. A basic distinction is made between injuries of the inner knee and those of the outer joint.

Runner's Knee

Runners frequently report pain in the outer region of the knee joint. This condition is often referred to as as "runner's knee". A runner's knee is characterised by the inflammation of a certain tendon that runs along the outside of the outer thigh. This tendon is part of a broad band of tendons (the *illio-tibial band*), which extends downward from one of the muscles of the outer thigh to the tibial plateau via the outer side of the thigh. During running, as the knee is bent and extended over and over again, it causes the illio-tibial band to rub against the bone. In combination with certain anatomical conditions, such as bow legs or knock-knees, the risk of overuse injuries in this area may be increased.

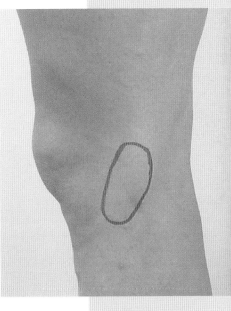

Pain in this spot, just above the joint space, is typical of runner's knee.

Patients suffering from runners knee may experience pain in the periosteum (the tissue that surrounds the bones except at the joints). It is also possible that a nearby bursa has been irritated by friction, resulting in pain. Typically, diffuse pain is first experienced in the outer knee, which may sometimes radiate up and down the leg. The main discomfort is usually

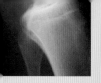

experienced two fingers above the outer joint space. Runner's knee problems do not affect the inner knee. Therefore, the joint itself is not irritated and it maintains full functionality. There is no fluid on the joint, and no sign of meniscus damage. If you experience pain in the outer knee, you should have a differential diagnostic check performed that rules out internal problems (e. g. abrasion or damage to the outer meniscus) or pain originating from the spine. It is the attending physician's responsibility to examine and assess these issues.

Pain in the Patellar Ligament

Certain forces acting upon the knee can cause stabbing pain, which makes it easy to diagnose a meniscus injury.

The patellar ligament (*ligamantum patellae*) transfers force from the extensor musculature of the thigh to the lower leg. When this ligament becomes irritated, pain is experienced primarily in the region of the tendon sheath (*tuberositas tibiae*) and/or just below the lower part of the kneecap (*apex patellae*). Both

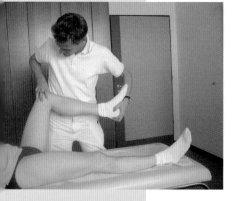

the ligament and the structures surrounding it can be inflamed. Small bursae act as shock absorbers and have a cushioning effect, supporting the patellar ligament. These bursae react to overuse with swelling and pain. Possible causes for this type of overuse injury are numerous and have to be assessed on a case-by-case basis. In many cases, counteracting an imbalance of the thigh muscles can lead to significant improvement.

Injuries of the Inner Knee

Compared to inflammations of the outer knee joint, injuries of the inner knee joint are encountered relatively rarely among runners. Even so, injuries of the inner knee (of the meniscus, for example) can occur as a result of a slight twist of the knee joint, or simply from overuse. Frequently, the meniscus already has a pre-existing weakness or defect, so that even slightly

abnormal load patterns can cause severe damage of the cartilaginous meniscus structure. In the long run, overuse can also lead to damage of the cartilage (arthrosis). The cartilage surface covering the articular surface (the place where two bones meet) is worn away by friction and can become thin or even progress to the point where the cartilage is worn off completely, causing great discomfort. Arthrosis can be brought about by excessive weight, by misalignment of the legs, by genetic factors or by past injuries of the knee joint.

2. Pain in the Achilles Tendon

The Achilles tendon, which connects the calf muscle with the heel bone, is the strongest tendon in the human body. It plays a major role in many athletic endeavours, and it is exposed to particularly high strain in disciplines that involve running and jumping. The increased risk of injuries to the Achilles tendon applies to both amateur and professional runners.

If you have trouble with your muscles, or especially the Achilles tendon, steep runs and uneven terrain should be enjoyed with caution. Better yet, avoid them altogether.

Injuries of the Achilles tendon are among the most common kinds of injuries sustained by runners. The symptoms, which frequently develop gradually and become chronic, include pain first thing in the morning until you have loosened up, and discomfort following exercise. As the symptoms progress, runners report experiencing pain during training, as well. In most cases, the discomfort seems quite harmless at first, with the result that the problem is often ignored, permitting it to progress to the point that regular training is no longer possible. Pain in the Achilles tendon can occur in various regions, including the area of the tendon itself, the tissue surrounding the tendon, the tendon sheath and the area in back of the Achilles tendon. Any pain in the Achilles tendon is often generically referred to as "achillodynia".

A good alternative to hill running is stair running. Because the steps are flat there is no additional pull or stretch acting on the tendons, and the training effect is about the same.

85

3. Runner's Hip

The condition referred to as runner's condition is mainly char-acterised by pain in the outer hip area. It is usually caused by an irritation of the bursa located over the greater trochanter, one of the surfaces at the top of the thighbone. The hip joint itself is not usually involved in runner's hip. The causes are numerous and have to be examined carefully to determine the appropriate therapeutic measures that will prevent a chronic inflammation of the bursa.

4. Stress Fractures and Periosteum Inflammation

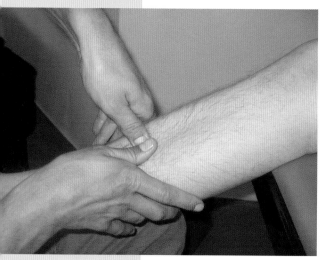

Our bones are part of the passive locomotor system and are designed to have a high degree of stability. Each bone consists of a hard outer layer (compacta) and a softer core, the cancellous bone (or spongiosa). A continuous process of bone growth and bone loss throughout our life makes it possible for our bones to adapt to varying demands.

Applying pressure across the shin is a painful, but effective, treatment for shin splints.

The periosteum is a layer of tissue that envelops the bone. It is highly vascularised and enervated, and therefore very sensitive. If there is a discrepancy between bone density and the stress placed on it, bone injuries may result. These injuries can be caused by sudden, massive impact of the kind which occurr in an accident. However, the identical demands repeated over and over again can also lead to bone damage. In such a situation we can observe stress reactions (e. g., inflammeation of the periostea or fluid retention within the bone) and even fatigue fractures. The latter consist in hairline fissures, which may be partial or complete. A lot of times, this type of fracture occurs in the lower extremities, especially in the shin, the fibula and the bones of the foot. Frequently stress fractures first cause a sensation of diffuse pain after exercise, which is often played down at first. Long-term pain, for example in connection with shin splints, can be the harbinger of a fatigue fracture in progress. This problem usually manifests itself in gradually intensifying pain, which occurs earlier and earlier on in your training sessions.

5. Plantar Fasciitis

*P*lantar fasciitis is a painful degeneration of the tendon that joins the heel and the ball of the foot. Pain is mainly experienced in the sole and near the heel, and is often – but not always correctly – attributed to hard calcium deposits on the heel commonly known as "heel spurs". Individual anatomy, improper running shoes and intensity of training are some of the factors that all contribute to overstressing the plantar fasciitis.

The plantar tendon runs along the sole of the foot. If you have a flatfoot or splayfoot and run barefoot, you run a higher risk of plantar fasciitis. Even so, you should train your foot arch by running barefoot and by doing some specific exercises (see page 76).

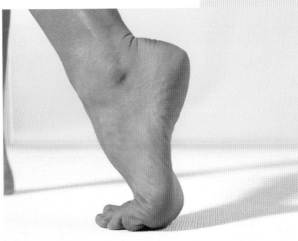

Therapy for Overuse Injuries

*A*side from an accurate diagnosis, the single most important therapy for this kind of injury is rest and relaxation.
Most overuse injuries are the result of overtraining, simply
pushing the body too hard. Therefore, it is important to adapt
your exercise programme to the condition of your musculoskeletal system, and to take advantage of alternative training
methods in place of the exercises that led to injury. Moreover,

*Unfortunately,
many an injury
that involves
inflammation
cannot be cured
without resorting to
pills or injections...*

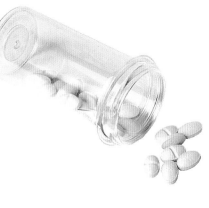

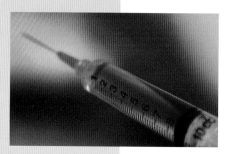

physical therapies (such as electrotherapy) and inflammation
inhibiting medications are available, both in the form of pills
and local applications. In the long term, of course, it is
important to identify and remedy the factors that caused the
injury so that it does not reoccur. A lot of times, this means
correcting your running technique and body position.

Muscular imbalances, for instance, can be treated by means of
physiotherapy. Feet that deviate significantly from an ideal
pronation (as described on page 26f) can be partially corrected
by using suitable inlays in running shoes.

And What if it Happens?
Alternative Training Methods –
Not Just When You're Injured!

What changes have been made in training methods in the past 10 to 15 years? Regenerative measures have been around for a long time. What has been added to the picture is alternative training methods that enable both amateur and professional runners to maintain a higher level of fitness for a longer period of time.

Twenty years ago, it was commonly assumed that cycling and swimming were detrimental to the runner's physical condition. The motion patterns were said to be too slow, leading to big, bulky muscles. Today, runners quite systematically use these sports as a fixed part of their training programme.

Aqua Jogging

Water or aqua jogging, a new alternative form of training, was sneered at just five to eight years ago. Many people in the pool with them thought the aqua joggers had special physical problems, or just didn't know how to swim. Today, many swimming pools offer wet vests or buoyancy belts (aids to keep your body upright so you can train against the resistance of water) for hire, and some even lend them at no cost. Older people have discovered the great benefits of this kind of exercise, too. Today, large groups of aqua joggers are panting away in the pools.

Aqua jogging is a great way to continue exercising after an injury.

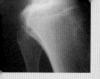

Advantages of aqua jogging: Movement pattern similar to running, but without ground contact, making it ideal during recovery from lower-body and feet injuries.

Disadvantage of aqua jogging with a wet vest: Since the vest provides buoyancy, you have to push yourself hard against the resistance of the water before your heart rate starts to climb. Self-discipline and motivation are required to not just relax in the water and let the vest interfere with your goals.

Beware!

Although alternative training methods can also stress the body, they involve less strain on tendons and ligaments than running, which is the main point: you can train your cardiovascular system without overtaxing your musculoskeletal system. This way, you can simulate an increase in your distance. Keep in mind the Golden Rule: a hard running session should be followed by an activity that promotes regeneration.

Cycling and Swimming

For everyone else, cycling and swimming should be a regular part of your training schedule – as a regenerative measure. These forms of exercise provide a moderate cardiovascular training in which you can give your tendons, joints and overused muscles a break, but at the same time you can increase the intensity of your workout as you see fit. This is particularly important after a high-intensity training session (tempo runs or a long run). Moreover, swimming strengthens all the muscles of the entire torso, so you can spare yourself a dry session or two at the gym. As a rule, a demanding workout should always

be followed by some form of alternative exercise. Make sure to keep the intensity low, so that you can complete the exercise without any great expenditure of effort. This gives the parts of your body greatly impacted by running a chance to recover while you still get a moderate cardiovascular workout, which

You don't have to go full throttle when spinning at the gym. Bikes can be adjusted so you can go easy and let your legs re-generate: let the flywheel do the work.

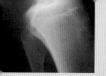

will help you to maintain your performance level in the mid-term. Alternative training is also the right answer anytime you don't feel like running. You're certainly familiar with those days when you just can't bear the thought of going for a run. But it still may be fun to go for an easy tour on the bike. Surprise your partner and your family and spend some quality time with them. Enjoy those days rather than forcing yourself to put on your running shoes and meet your mileage quota. Another thing to do at such time is to take a long walk, enjoying the beauty of nature together with your partner. This is active relaxation, and far better than going for a run against your will, wondering why it refuses to go smoothly.

Possible Forms of Regeneration Training:

- 30 minutes to 1.5 hours of cycling at the most relaxed pace imaginable, if possible without hills. You might want to do this in your normal casual clothes, or with an old bicycle, so that you won't even be tempted to compete with groups of cyclists who happen to pass you by.

- 20–30 minutes of swimming, focusing on the arm strokes, preferably freestyle with your legs kicking gently. Switch between swimming styles every once in a while. Try the backstroke, for instance.

- Hiking or walking anywhere from half an hour to two hours, as long as you want, without any particular predetermined time or distance to achieve.

Cross-Country Skiing and Skating

One of the best and most effective alternatives to running has always been cross-country skiing, whether it's ski skating or the traditional diagonal stride. Cross-country skiing involves hip extension and, on uphill sections, trains the leg extensors (experiment to find your pressure point). The cardiovascular effects are stunning, while the regeneration phase is very short in relation to the intensity of the workout. In cross-country skiing, your heart rate is about 20 beats higher and you can continue about 1.5 times as long as if you were running. The higher pulse is caused by the fact that the arms and the trunk are involved to a greater extent, which also means that these muscles are better trained than in running. Downhill passages give your legs some rest every once in a while. Finally, there are no impact shocks as in running.

Cross-country skiing is one of the best alternatives to running.

Some gyms have good cross-trainers that simulate the motion of cross-country skiing. Of course, they can't recreate the mar vellous winter scenery.

Skating with roller skates or in-line skates offers advantages similar to cross-country skiing. Without using poles, it is more like ice speed skating. Recently, skating has also been combined with poles, which makes the movement pattern very similar to that of ski skating. However, beware: if you should fall down, you won't land in the soft snow, but on hard asphalt. Many a skater has experienced a painful graze or a bruised tailbone, ruling out running for a while. Never go skating without the protection of kneepads, elbow pads, and wrist protectors.

The Gym

The best gyms have long since shed their body building image and have turned into true cardic factories. Frequently, today's gyms boast dozens o treadmills, cross-trainers, ergonomic bikes, rowing machines and much more.

Sources of Information on Performance Diagnosis Services in the UK*

Sport England
Victoria House
Bloomsbury Square
London
WC1B 4SE
Tel: 020 7273 1500
Fax: 020 7383 5740
Website: www.sportengland.org

English Institute of Sport
Central London Office
Tel: 0870 759 0410
Website for all UK branches:
www.eis2win.co.uk

Crystal Palace National Sports Centre
English Institute of Sport
Ledrington Road
London SE19 2BB
Tel: 0870 759 0410

English Institute of Sport
University of Bath
Claverton Down
Bath BA2 7AY
Tel: 01225 384 441

English Institue of Sport
Sportcity, Manchester
Gate 13
Rowsley Street
Manchester M11 3FF
Tel: 0161 231 8602

English Institute of Sport
Sportpark, University of East Anglia
Norwich
Norfolk NR4 7TJ
Tel: 0163 59 3329
Website: www.sportspark.co.uk

Sport England East
English Institute of Sport
Crescent House
19 The Crescent
Bedford
MK40 2QP
Tel: 08458 508 508
Fax: 01234 359046

Sheffield Centre of Sports Medicine
5 Broomfield Road
Broomhill
Sheffield S10 2SE
Tel: 0114 267 8889
Website: www.shef.ac.uk/dcss/scsm
Sports Medicine Clinic
University of Bristol
Tyndall Avenue
Bristol BS8 1TP
Tel: 0117 928 8810
Fax: 0117 331 1105
Website:
www.bris.ac.uk/sport/sportsmedicine/

Sports Council for Northern Ireland
House of Sport
Upper Malone Road
Belfast
BT9 5LA
Tel: 028 9038 1222
Fax: 028 9068 2757

Scottish Institute of Sport
Caledonia House
South Gyle
Edinburgh
EH12 9DQ
Tel: 0131 317 7200
Fax: 0131 317 720

Sport Scotland
Caledonia House
South Gyle
Edinburgh
EH12 9DQ
Tel / Fax: 0131-317 7200
Website: www.sportscotland.org.uk

Sports Council for Wales
Welsh Institute of Sport
Sophia Gardens
Cardiff
CF1 9SW
Tel: 029 2030 0500
Fax: 029 2030 0600
Website: www.sports-council-wales.co.uk

The National Sports Medicine Institute
of the United Kingdom
32 Devonshire Street
London W1G 6PX
Tel: 020 7908 3636
Fax: 020 7908 3635

British Association of Sport and
Exercise Medicine
BASEM Office
PO Box 148
Chelsea Close
Amperley Road
Armley
Leeds LS12 4WW
Tel: 0113 263 5014
Website: www.basem.co.uk

British Association of Sport and
Exercise Sciences
Leeds Metropolitan University
Carnegie Faculty of Sport and Education
Fairfax Hall
Headingley Campus, Beckett Park
Leeds LS6 3QS
Tel / Fax: 0113 283 6162
Website: www.bases.org.uk

List of sports injury clinics online at
www.sportsinjuryclinic.net

*The information given here is intended to be a starting point to help you find facilities offering sports science and sports medical services in your area. In addition, many physicians can offer some of these services. This list is in no way intended to be complete.

INDEX